GRUESOME FACTS

igloo

Published in 2010
By Igloo Books Ltd
Cottage Farm
Sywell
NN6 0BJ

www.igloo-books.com

B044 0810

10 9 8 7 6 5 4 3 2 1

ISBN 978 1 84852 982 3
Printed and manufactured in China

INTRODUCTION

Did you know that the smelly, mucus-laden bootlace worm which lives around the coast can grow to an incredible 60m (200ft) long, or that the hardest thing to clean out of a sewer is not poo but big lumps of fat? Can you believe that all the Romans who used the same public toilet wiped their bottoms with the same sponge on a stick, or that Parmesan cheese and vomit smell very similar because they both contain one particular acid? Did you know that during the Siege of Colchester, people ate cats, rats, and candlewax to stay alive, that polar bears can go all winter without doing a poo, and that a woman once grew her fingernails 90cm (35in) long?!

Welcome to *Gruesome Facts*. It's a gruesome world out there, and we've scoured the four corners of it to bring you the most horrible and grisly deeds and doings you'll ever read about in your life. Quite simply, this book is a compendium of amazing ghastliness. The dictionary defines gruesome as "inspiring repugnance and horror." We've added another layer by only including stories with an extra eeuuugh! factor.

That means they're guaranteed to inform, fascinate – and churn your stomach at the same time!

You'll find gruesome facts about an extraordinary range of topics, like the Worst Animal Bloodsuckers, Horrid Medical Cures, Nasty Bodily Excretions, Scary Sports, Slithering Snakes, Sticky Ends, and different nations' appetites for tasty delicacies such as deep-fried tarantulas and dog's liver. How hideous can hair be? What are Rotten Smells made up of?

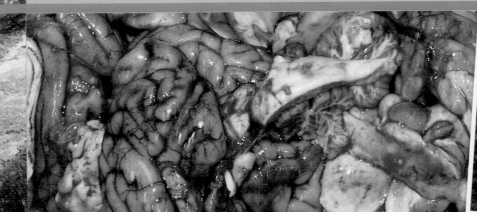

Do you know what Strange Bathing Habits people have around the world, or how long hairballs can exist for in the human intestine?

We give you the wackiest, the most gruesome facts and figures on topics including the Natural World, the Body, the Animal Kingdom, Food, and Sport. We've got sections on History, including Nasty Rulers and Evil Empires, bloodthirsty Vikings, and ghastly Plagues and Epidemics. Keeping up with the world of experiments and discoveries, there are special pages on Medicine and Science, including Gross Experiments, Fantastic Forensics, and Troublesome Technology. For instance, did you know that computers can suddenly burst into flames while sitting on your desk? We've also found incredibly horrible stories about the paranormal world of vampires, zombies, witches, and aliens, and have tracked down Ghostly Graveyards and other spooky places.

All in all, *Gruesome Facts* brings together the world's goriest, ghastliest, grimmest, and most disgusting events, facts, human achievements, and natural happenings in one impressively jam-packed book. It is amazing, horrifying, and truly, awfully gruesome. So let's get going!

ANIMAL WORLD

HISTORY

URBAN LIVING

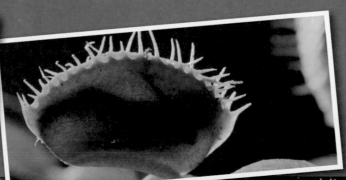

SPORT

FOOD

SCIENCE & MEDICAL

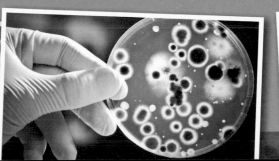

PARANORMAL

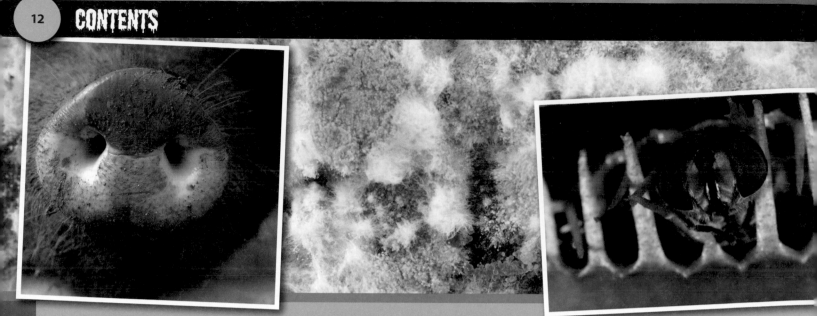

NATURAL WORLD

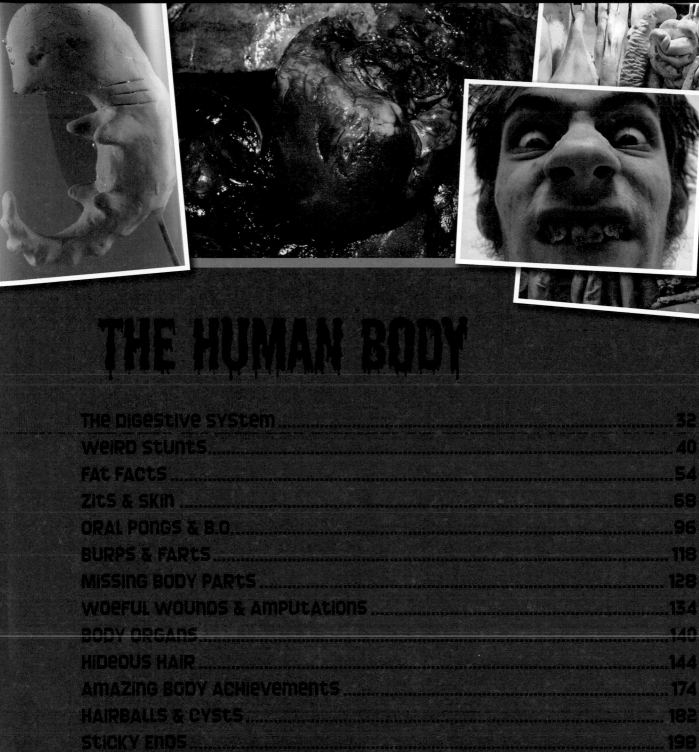

THE HUMAN BODY

PYTHON BLOCKS TOILET

In 2006, a large python was found peering out of a toilet bowl in Howard Springs, Australia. The toilet had blocked and when a plumber investigated he found a porky 2.1m (7ft) carpet python staring up at him. It had been living in the septic tank and curled its long body through the S-bend.

SLITHERING SPA

At Ada Barak's carnivorous plant farm in Israel you can experience the most bizarre spa treatment ever – a deep-tissue snake massage. Slithering non-venomous serpents are let loose to writhe over your back, shoulders, and face. The larger king and corn snakes give your muscles a good knead, while smaller garden varieties have a soothing and calming touch.

WORLD'S MOST VENOMOUS

The Fierce Snake or Inland Taipan of Australia is the world's most venomous snake – the toxin released in just one bite is enough to kill 100 people or 250,000 small mammals, such as rats and mice, its favorite food.

VENOM IN YOUR EYE

So-called spitting cobras are hugely successful at shooting blinding venom into the eyes of their prey – at a distance of 60cm (23.6in), they rarely miss. That's because they don't actually spit, they spray. Just before they force the venom through their fangs, the cobras jerk their heads fast from side to side, creating a wide pattern of spray that maximizes their chance of hitting their attacker in the eye.

DEAD SNAKE BITES BACK

Never pick up a dead snake – even after they are decapitated, they can give a venomous bite. One man in Washington State, USA, severed a 1.5m (5ft) rattlesnake in two, then bent down to pick up its body parts. The severed head moved and bit the man's finger. Scientists think that snakes' heat-seeking and reflex-bite abilities still work for a short time after they have died.

THE TITANOBOA WEIGHED MORE THAN A CAR!

SPINE-TINGLING!
THE INLAND TAIPAN'S BITE IS ENOUGH TO KILL 100 PEOPLE!

HISS-TORIC MONSTER

The biggest snake yet found on earth is the Titanoboa – a prehistoric super-constrictor that was longer than a bus, heavier than a car, and devoured giant turtles whole. This super-predator lived about 60 million years ago. Scientists estimate that this 13m- (42.6ft-) long reptile weighed 1,134kg (2,500lb), and would find it hard to squeeze through the front door of a house.

NOSE SNAKES

As a party trick, this takes some beating! Manoharan, alias "Snake Manu," from Chennai in India can pull live snakes through his mouth and out through his nostrils. When he was 13, he started practicing by threading the snakes through the passage at the back of the mouth and into his nasal cavity. He's tried tree snakes, kraits, cobras, sand boas, and rat snakes and, astonishingly, has been bitten only a few times.

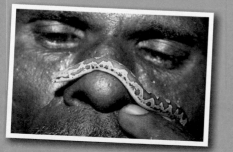

GATOR-EATING SNAKE EXPLODES!

A 4m (13ft) python exploded when it tried to swallow a live 1.8m (6ft) alligator whole. The gory remains of the two predators were found in the Florida swamplands after their battle to the death – the alligator's hindquarters were protruding from the Burmese python's midsection, while its head, shoulders, and front legs remained inside the snake. It's thought that the alligator may have clawed its way through the python's stomach while it was being digested alive.

HORRORS!
AROUND 1 MILLION GLADIATORS LOST THEIR LIVES IN THE RING.

FIGHT OR DIE

Life was tough for Roman soldiers, who had to join the army for 25 years. If they badly injured an arm or leg, it was cut off without any anaesthetic, and if they deserted they would be beaten or stoned to death. Many of the soldiers were not Romans. They were foreigners who had been captured in battle and forced to join the army. If they refused, they were executed.

DANGEROUS FOR GIRLS

It wasn't fun being a girl in Roman times. Most men did not want girls to even learn how to read and they were often forced to marry at the age of 14. Worse still, many girls were killed at birth because families only wanted to have male heirs.

WANT A LARK?

For a special treat, Romans used to eat larks' tongues. The lark is only a little bird, so it must have taken hundreds of their tongues to fill up a hungry Roman. Other grisly delicacies that were eaten at banquets included roasted dormouse, flamingo, ostrich brains, and stinking rotten-fish sauce.

MISSING IN THE FOREST

The Roman Army was the best in the world and killed hundreds of thousands of people as the Empire spread through Europe, the Middle East, and North Africa. They killed up to 80,000 Britons in just one battle with Queen Boudicca. Sometimes, though, they met their match: in AD9, three legions went into the Black Forest in Germany and disappeared. No one knows what happened to them, but piles and piles of bones were later found.

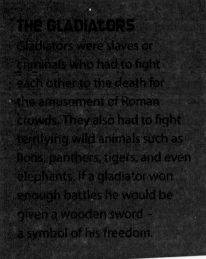

NERO CLAUDIUS CAESAR AUGUSTUS GERMANICUS

THE GLADIATORS

Gladiators were slaves or criminals who had to fight each other to the death for the amusement of Roman crowds. They also had to fight terrifying wild animals such as lions, panthers, tigers, and even elephants. If a gladiator won enough battles he would be given a wooden sword – a symbol of his freedom.

THE VOMIT-COLLECTORS

The Romans loved to eat and drink so much that they used to vomit so that they could consume even more. Usually they would not even leave the dining room and would be sick on the floor, but some houses had a special room called a vomitorium. Emperor Claudius would tickle the inside of his throat with a feather to make himself throw up. A vomit-collecting slave would have to clear up the mess.

KILLING SPREE

Emperor Nero killed his own mother, Agrippina, and his first wife, Octavia. He cut off his wife's head and sent it as a present to his new girlfriend, Poppea. But he soon went off her and killed her as well. He also liked killing people by covering them with tar and burning them alive, crucifying them, or feeding them to wild dogs.

THE EMPEROR MUST DIE

The Romans were very fond of killing their political rivals, and even their own family members. In AD3, there were 20 different emperors in just 50 years – most of them were murdered. Julius Caesar was the most famous Roman leader to be assassinated. In 44BC he was stabbed 23 times by his colleagues, including Brutus, who he thought was his friend.

VERY PUBLIC TOILETS

There was no privacy in public toilets. They just consisted of a long bench with a row of holes in it, so everyone would have to sit together in a line. There wasn't any toilet paper, either. The Romans would use a wet sponge on a stick.

RANCID!

Have you ever noticed that Parmesan cheese and sick have a very similar smell? It's stomach-churning, but with a slight sweet edge to it. That's because both contain butyric acid, which is found in rancid butter and body odor too. Its powerful rancid smell is very attractive to animals and fish, and is often added by fishermen to their bait to tempt fishes to bite.

HOUSEHOLD HORROR!

The sharp, pungent aroma of ammonia has most people gagging, but you smell it often around the house – in cleaning products, cat's pee, and sometimes even in human sweat. Before the 20th century, household ammonia was derived from animal poo, including camel dung. Nowadays, it's more likely to be chemically produced.

CORPSE FLOWERS

Some pongy flowers smell of decaying flesh, which is why they're called corpse flowers. There are many varieties living all over the world, from Indonesia to South Africa and the U.S.A. Flesh-eating flies and beetles love their stink and race toward the flowers as soon as they release their putrid aroma. The reek is caused by putrescine and cadaverine, two chemical compounds which smell just as bad as their names suggest.

BAD EGG!

One of the nastiest smells around is that of bad eggs. This foul odor pops up in a surprising number of places – in blocked drains and sewers, in swamps, hot springs and volcanoes, in rotten eggs (of course) and even in the human gut! It's due to a chemical compound called hydrogen sulfide that's made when living things decay in places where there's not much oxygen. Like swamps or drains…

THE GODZILLA OF ODORS

The foulest aroma in the world makes people want to vomit when they smell it. It's been called "repulsive," "an assault on the senses," "the Godzilla of odors," and "extremely distressing." Opening up a jar of this horrible stuff will foul up the air in a room for days. Luckily, most of us will never smell it: it's created by chemicals called isonitriles, and only a few people working in specialist chemical labs will ever be exposed to its noxious fumes.

STAR JELLY

When shooting stars hit Earth, people often report foul-smelling blobs of jelly lying around afterwards. Star jelly has been known about since the 1400s, and examples have been investigated for years. After a Perseid meteor shower in 1979, one woman in Texas complained of three purple, plum-pudding blobs on her front yard, which were taken off for analysis. But a 2009 outbreak of star jelly in Scotland still has scientists baffled. Some people think the goo is regurgitated frog or toad bits, dropped by birds, though when scientific tests were done, the mucous had no plant or animal origins. The smelly mystery continues.

SWEET, THEN SOUR!

How weird is this? The chemical compound indole has a sweet, flowery aroma at low concentrations but in higher doses it smells just like poo. It's used in perfume and cosmetics to give an orange blossom or jasmine scent, but it's also found in human poop and helps give it that trademark pong!

CHILDREN & BEARS

Children have a better sense of smell than adults, dogs have a better sense of smell than children, and bears have the best sense of smell of all. It's thought that bears can smell food in the air from 15 or more miles away – and they use their sniff skills to pinpoint rotting flesh buried in caves or underground.

INSECTS IN THE USA

Insects are cheap, nutritious, and high in protein – crickets, mealworms, small grasshoppers, and giant water beetles contain around 20g protein per 100g (0.7oz per 3.5oz), almost as much as a steak. At some North American universities where they study insects, they're trying to make bug-eating more popular by devising new insect recipes. For example, to make crunchy Banana Worm Bread, just add ¼ cup dry-roasted army worms to your normal recipe.

NEARLY **1,500** DIFFERENT TYPES OF INSECTS ARE EATEN AROUND THE WORLD.

LIVE MAGGOT CHEESE

"Casu marzu" is a traditional Italian cheese riddled with thousands of live maggots and left to ferment for three months until it turns runny and very smelly. People eat the cheese spread on flatbread with the maggots still alive, though they have to cover their eyes and nose as the tiny translucent worms often launch themselves up to 15cm (6in) in protest. It's best to crunch the maggots to death before swallowing a casu marzu sandwich, as once they've found their way into the intestines, their sharp mouth-hooks can tear holes in the gut.

WITCHETTY GRUBS

In the Australian outback, it's a great treat to eat live witchetty grubs straight from the ground. These fat, fleshy, giant moth caterpillars grow to about 15cm (6in) long and have runny insides with a sweetish almond flavor. They can also be cooked in ashes until the skin crusts and the meat turns light yellow, when they're said to taste nutty and creamy!

HACHI-NO-KO

Japanese Emperor Hirohito's favorite traditional food was said to be hachi-no-ko – boiled or fried wasp larvae – served on a bed of rice. The wasps are driven from their nests by firecrackers, then the larvae are collected by hand and cooked with soy sauce and sugar. They taste slightly sweet with a light crunchy texture.

BARBECUED DRAGONFLIES

Dragonflies and damselflies are dipped in coconut oil, barbecued over a hot grill, then eaten as a high-protein snack in the Indonesian island of Bali.

CRUNCHY TARANTULAS

In country markets in Cambodia, you'll always find big pots of deep-fried tarantulas (usually next to the deep-fried grasshoppers) which locals munch on for a treat. The legs are crunchy, the head tastes like fishy chicken, but the soft round abdomen is considered the gourmet bit – it contains the spider's lungs, heart, and excrement in a dark brown mushy paste.

ANT CAVIAR

Mexican diners often start a meal with a tortilla filled with ant eggs, guacamole, and tomato salsa. The eggs, known as escamoles, are harvested from round the roots of agave plants, then boiled until they are soft and white. They taste creamy and buttery, rather like soft cheese.

YUK!
THAT'S DISGUSTING.

FAST-FOOD WORMS

Koreans are famous for eating dog meat soup but as a snack they prefer silkworm pupae, a delicacy called beondegi. You can buy these little creatures in paper cupfuls from street vendors or in tins from supermarkets. Boiled, they look like fat maggots and taste a bit like wet leaves; deep fried and well-seasoned, they're crunchy and meatier.

BLACK SCORPION SOUP

In this nasty looking soup, 30 to 40 live black scorpions are quickly flash fried then tossed into a boiling broth with some pork meat, ginger, and garlic. This is a delicacy from the Yunnan Province of China, and helps to keep the local scorpion population down.

WOW!
THE GERMAN SUBMARINE U-1206 SANK IN 1945 WHEN ITS TOILET WAS OPERATED IMPROPERLY.

SINK SPOT

The grimiest spot in a public toilet or restroom is not the toilet seat where people bare their bottoms or the flush handle which they touch immediately after doing their business. It's actually the sink. Sink areas are damp and warm so are teeming with gruesome bacteria.

BIG SMELL

The River Thames in London was always used as the city's sewer. But the smell got so bad in the hot summer of 1858 that there was a public outcry about the so-called Great Stink. As a result, London's massive underground sewerage system was built by 1875. Lots of people used to work in the sewers, including "flushers," who flushed away built-up piles of waste, "toshers," who searched the sewers for valuables, and "rat-catchers," who killed the rats that could cause disease.

FAT BLOCKAGE

The worst thing for blocking up sewers is not poo, but fat. When fat is liquid, some people pour it down their sinks to get rid of it. But as soon as it gets cool in the sewers it solidifies and blocks the passageways. Sewer workers have to crawl through the tunnels and flush the solid waxy fat away with high-pressure jets. Sometimes the fat builds up into such huge wodges it has to be chipped off by hand with pick-axes instead.

LID DOWN

After pooing, it's more hygienic to flush the toilet with the lid down. Flushing with the lid up allows a plume of bacteria-laden water vapor to escape from the toilet bowl into the bathroom's atmosphere. It floats around for a few hours before coming to land – on surfaces including your toothbrush! To avoid swallowing splattered droplets full of nasty germs, some people hide their toothbrushes in the bathroom cupboard.

Ancient FLUSH

Amazingly, a system of flushing toilets was in use around 2,600BC. In the ancient city of Mohenjo-Daro in today's Pakistan, where 35,000 people lived, almost every house had a bathroom and a water-flushed toilet connected to sewers which ran below the streets. The toilets were built on the street side of the walls: they had brick or wooden seats, and people's poo dropped through a chute in the wall, and was flushed with water into the sewers. These early sewer systems were quite smelly, because there was often a gap between the chute and the sewer, so all manner of odors and other gruesome stuff could escape.

GARDYLOO!

In the olden days, streets were running sewers. People used to chuck "night soil" – the overnight wee and poo from their chamber pot – out into the road every morning from their windows. They'd shout "Gardyloo!" (from the French "Gardez l'eau!" or "Beware, water!") to warn people to get out of the way. The only drains were gutters in the road which flowed into rivers, polluting them. It wasn't until the late 18th century that people started to have rooms with toilets, called water closets.

MATTER OF TASTE

Different countries like different-shaped loo pans and flush systems. In Germany, poo is often dropped onto a flat porcelain surface, before being flushed away with a powerful jet of water. For many years in France, people pooped squatting into porcelain holes in the ground. And in Japan, they have high-tech, remote-controlled toilets with heated seats that first wash your bottom, then blow-dry it.

Enfield Poltergeist

In 1977, investigators studied the Enfield Poltergeist, which was said to be tormenting the Hodgson family from Enfield, north London. The family believed it moved huge pieces of furniture across the floor, scribbled on walls, caused puddles, cold breezes, and spontaneous fires, tore a fireplace from the wall, flung crockery, books, pictures, and even the children around. The supernatural phenomena were seen by over 30 different witnesses including a policewoman who signed a statement saying she'd seen a chair move by itself. The poltergeist apparently "talked" through one of the children, saying his name was Bill and he'd died in the sitting room chair – facts later found to be true.

Demon Drummer

One of the earliest known poltergeists was the Drummer of Tedworth. In 1661 it apparently inhabited the house of magistrate John Mompesson, and for the next two years was said to bang out marching tunes on the doors, roof, and children's bedsteads for two hours a night. Then the family reported that it became even more mischievous, throwing plates, shoes, clothes, and furniture around the room. Everyone said it arrived with a "hurling" of air, and often left a nasty sulfurous smell behind.

A Nasty Way to Go

The Bell Witch was a very nasty poltergeist that is said to have terrorized the Bell family of Tennessee. It seemed to like making human noises – laughing, gulping, choking, coughing, lip-smacking – and would slap the children's faces and pull their hair. Some said it shouted obscenities, and would throw furniture and food around. After three years' torment, John Bell, the father of the family, was apparently found dead one morning with a strange bottle of smoky brown liquid beside him. The poltergeist is said to have confessed to poisoning him, and a little later it disappeared.

MIND OVER MATTER?

In the 1970s, U.S. lab technician Felicia Parise used to give demonstrations in which she was reported to move small objects like pill boxes, compass needles, and glasses using the power of her mind alone – just like a poltergeist. It's said that this feat took such intense concentration that she'd sweat profusely, her heart would race, and she'd lose a couple of pounds in weight.

SPOOKILY WELL-DRESSED

A destructive poltergeist was said to live in the Phelps Mansion in Stratford, Connecticut during the 1850s. During the day, people saw clothes and other objects sailing around the house, windows would break, and furniture dance. The nights were reportedly full of strange knockings, screams, and voices. But the most unnerving apparitions were the lifesize effigies of 20 or so women praying, kneeling, or standing – it's said they were all wearing Mrs. Phelps' clothes.

SUPERNATURAL FIRES

In the Sicilian village of Canneto di Caronia in 2004, people's cookers, mobile phones, lamps, refrigerators, electric cables, and furniture started spontaneously bursting into flames. No one's discovered why, though many suspect poltergeists…

PARANORMAL POWERS

Ever since someone broke into the burial vault of cruel Scottish lawyer George Mackenzie in 1998, visitors to the Edinburgh churchyard where he lies are said to have been attacked by something invisible. Over 500 people report being hit, pinched, scratched, bitten, gouged, or bruised. An exorcist was brought in to get rid of the malignant force but gave up, saying it was so strong it could kill him. A few weeks later, he is said to have died.

MOVING DOLLS

One Bavarian poltergeist was rumored to like nothing more than moving dolls around the house. The family said that they would see their dolls floating round corners and along the corridors, then being placed gently down in another room. Even when the dolls were locked away in cupboards, they'd somehow rematerialize somewhere else the next day.

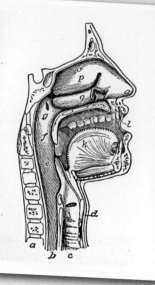

WOW! SURGEONS WERE DRILLING HOLES IN PEOPLE'S SKULLS IN 6,000BC.

EYE-WATERING OP

It's astonishing that 2,500 years ago, surgeons were operating on cataracts in the eye and people were living to tell the tale. But cataract "couching" – a gruesome procedure in which the cloudy cataract lens was pushed down inside the eyeball by a curved needle – was described by a Hindu doctor around 400BC. After the op, he suggested soothing the area with warm clarified butter and a bandage.

WINDPIPE WIZARDRY

In 1620, a 14-year-old boy swallowed a bag of gold coins to stop them being stolen, but they got stuck at the back of his throat and he was unable to breathe. French surgeon Nicholas Habicot described how he quickly cut a hole in the boy's windpipe to clear his airways – one of the earliest examples of a "tracheotomy" – thereby saving his life. Then he eased the bag past the stomach opening so it could work its way through his system and the gold coins would come out the other end.

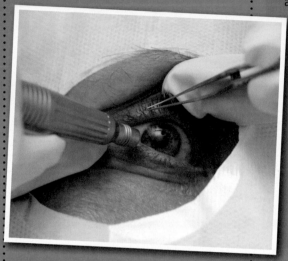

THAT MUST HURT!

Visiting the dentist for a filling may have been almost as common 9,000 years ago as it is today. In prehistoric graves in Pakistan's Indus valley, some people were found to have had their molars drilled (without painkillers – ouch!) with holes up to 3.5mm (0.1in) deep.

FIRST NOSE JOB

Ancients often got their noses cut off in battle, but as early as 400BC surgeons were able to fashion them new ones. They'd cut a leaf-shaped flap of skin from the center of the person's forehead (making sure they left some skin attached above the bridge to supply blood to the new nose). The flap was twisted down over two bamboo tubes which became the nostrils. Gradually the new nose grafted on to the face, though how good it looked is anyone's guess.

BELIEVE IT... OR NOT

One of the ancient world's most famous operations was the leg transplant reputedly performed by twin doctors Cosmas and Damian in the 4th century AD. They apparently removed a Roman's gangrenous leg above the knee and grafted on the leg of an Ethiopian who had just died. When the man woke, he was amazed to find he had two good legs. Sounds incredible!

NEW EARLOBE, ANYONE?

The ancients' earlobes often got stretched an inch or more from wearing heavy earrings, but it was an easy job for surgeons to remove this unsightly ear dangle. First the lobe was chopped horizontally to a normal length, then the edges were sewn round neatly.

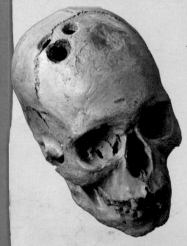

SKULL DRILLING

The oldest surgery in the world is also one of the most gruesome – cutting pieces of bone out of the skull, otherwise known as trepanning. Hundreds of prehistoric skulls have holes drilled in them, though no one is quite sure why. Maybe it relieved pressure on the brain caused by head wounds, or was a way to release "evil" spirits. The biggest danger was taking out chunks of the brain as well, though it seems many people lived long enough after the operation for the bone edge to heal over.

DOWN THE MOUNTAIN

Some people go down huge mountains on unicycles. They have to jump from rock face to cliff to scree, avoiding crevices and vertical drops, on a machine that has one wheel and no brakes. One man almost completely severed his foot when it slipped into the spokes of his speeding unicycle wheel in wet weather. His foot was only held on by strands of soft tissue and he needed emergency surgery to save it.

BARE-KNUCKLE BOXING

Before gloves were used to protect hands, boxers used to fight "bare-knuckled" and would end up with bruised hands and very bloody bodies. Their bouts would go on until one of the contestants was knocked out or dropped from exhaustion. In 1889, America's last professional bare-knuckle boxing match lasted an incredible 75 rounds – that's 3 hours 45 minutes. The match was between notorious Boston brawler John L. Sullivan and Jake Kilrain. Sullivan won, after Kilrain threw in the sponge, worried he'd die if the fight went on a moment longer.

SICK-MAKING ZORB

Zorbing is the sport most likely to make you upchuck instantly. Two people are harnessed facing each other inside a 3m (10ft) high, see-through ball, with arms and legs outstretched. The ball is rolled down a long hill with the zorbonauts inside turning head over heels at speeds of up to 56kph (35mph) all the way to the bottom. The fast twirling and whirling can make people vomit, with the likelihood of spraying each other all over with chunky stuff at every stomach-churning turn.

MOB SOCCER

The first English soccer games were like massed battles between huge numbers of neighboring villagers, using an inflated pig's bladder as a ball. The bladder could be kicked, carried, or thrown and the first "team" to drag it to a certain marker line – often miles away from each other – were the winners. In the Middle Ages, these games were traditionally played on Shrove Tuesday (Pancake Day) and would leave the village devastated and many of the players with cuts, wounds, and broken bones.

BASE JUMPING

Stepping off a 305m (1,000ft) cliff, BASE jumpers have just a second or two to open their parachute before crashing to the ground. They jump from 4 types of objects – Buildings, Antennae (radio masts), Span (bridges), and Earth (cliffs), which is where the name BASE comes from. BASE jumping is a fatally dangerous activity. In 2002, 1 in 60 people who tried it killed themselves by crashing into rocks or other obstructions or because the parachute failed to open in time.

BLOW UP!

Hand-grenade throwing used to be recognized as a sport in the Far East. Schoolchildren in the 1950s to 1970s practiced it alongside running, skipping, and tug-of-war, though thankfully the grenades they used weren't live.

CAVE DIVING

This is one of the spookiest sports you can do. Divers have to find their way through hideously deep depths in pitch-black caves with a limited air supply – perhaps meeting vicious creatures hiding in the waters along the way. It's lethally dangerous too, with one of the highest death rates of any sport.

THE BIG CATS

The big killer cats (lions, tigers, leopards, and jaguars) are the most powerful mammal predators. Best not to look when they're eating. Combining agility and strength, they tackle their target to the ground, and either suffocate their prey with a throat-bite, or bite on the spinal column to make a clean kill.

VICIOUS KILLER

AWESOME TIGER

The tiger is the largest of the big cats. The Siberian tiger grows up to 3.3m (11ft) long and weighs up to 300kg (660lb). The tiger's major asset is its power. Its strength enables it to hunt and kill other large mammals, including the buffalo, boar, and camel. Sometimes, a tiger will even fight an adult elephant. It bites the throat of its victim and uses its powerful forelegs to hold it down until it suffocates.

MAN-EATERS

Tigers have killed more humans than any other big cat. Occasionally, a tiger gets a taste for humans and starts to prey on villagers. These tigers are usually quite old. They pick on humans because we are slower, less agile, and have fewer natural defenses than most large animals in the wild.

MOST VICIOUS KILLER?

Surprisingly, perhaps the most vicious of all cats is the humble house cat. It is the only cat that hunts for fun. Lions, tigers, and all the big cats hunt in order to feed themselves, but the house cat is usually fed well by its human owner. Nevertheless, most of them really enjoy hunting, and their victims include thousands of species of animals and insects, including mice, birds, and fish.

FAStest Cat

The cheetah is the fastest animal on land. It reaches speeds of 120kph (75mph). It chases its prey down and usually trips it up by swiping at its legs. It then sets to work with its teeth, severing the arteries of the throat. Its common prey is the gazelle, but sometimes cheetahs will work in packs to bring down an adult zebra.

American Big Cat

The only one of the 4 big cat species that lives in North America is the jaguar. It is the third largest of the big cats and has an incredibly powerful bite that can rip through its prey. The jaguar has an unusual, brutal way of killing its victims. It bites through the skull and pierces the brain. The cat then eats the heart and lungs first.

The Spotted Cat

The spotted leopard is the smallest of the four big cat species, and has to look over its shoulder just in case a lion is coming. A lion will sometimes steal a leopard's prey, and will kill leopard cubs if it gets the chance. In order to get away from predatory lions, leopards have learnt how to scrabble up trees very quickly while still clinging on to their prey. A few leopards have become man-eaters.

Feline Fighting

Lions fight each other to the death to prove their supremacy, only living until they are about 10 as a result. The male lion sets out to become the head of a "pride" comprising female lions and a few other males. Lions often hunt together, stalking and circling their prey – including buffalo, zebra, and wildebeest – before leaping on them and killing them, either through strangulation, or a swipe of their paw.

ACID ATTACK

The acids in your tummy have a pH of around 2 – so strong they can dissolve metals, and could make holes in the wall of your stomach. So why don't they? Luckily for us, the stomach is lined with very thick layers of mucus which replace themselves every three days. These stop the tummy from digesting itself.

GUT LENGTH!

The human digestive tract seems long at about 8m (26ft) but that's nothing. A horse's food tube is around 27m (89ft) long, and that of a manatee or sea cow is around 30m (98ft)! These two are herbivores that eat mostly grasses and water plants. Plant food takes a long time to be broken down into good things the body can use, which is why herbivores' guts are extra-long.

WAY TO GO!

Food takes a very twisty path through our bodies. It starts in the mouth, gets chewed up into bits, then passes down the gullet and into the stomach. Food in the stomach is treated rough; it's like being tossed in a storm while getting rained down on by nasty acid. Eventually the food is reduced to a kind of soupy mush and heads off into the intestines where the goodness is extracted and the rest is processed by billions of bacteria. The last stop is your bottom, where all the waste is eliminated as poo…

SPIT IT OUT!

Humans produce somewhere between 0.75–1.5l (1–2½pt) of saliva every day. That's an awful lot of slobber! Why? Because it keeps the mouth nice and healthy, but also kickstarts the process of breaking down food.

STOMACH THiS

People eat the stomachs of cow, sheep, and ox. It's called tripe, and it is white with deep honeycomb shapes in it. In Turkey, there are special tripe restaurants which stay open all night, and tripe soup is a famous delicacy, if you can stomach it!

TUMMY RUMBLES

When you're hungry, or sometimes when you lie down, your tummy can start rumbling violently. This is gas being squished and squashed by strong muscles in the stomach and intestines. These noises have the most brilliant name – they're called borborygmi, just don't ask us how to pronounce it!

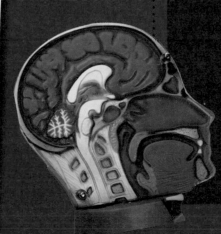

USELESS BiT?

Where the small and large intestines meet, there is a strange hollow tube. It's called the appendix and no one is quite sure why it's there. It can get blocked by lumpy waste and swell up with pus. It can even burst – which is called a ruptured appendix – when it has to be removed by an operation. The appendix is normally about the size of a finger, but the largest ever recorded measured a whopping 26cm (10in).

DOWN THE HATCH

When you swallow, food goes through a trap door into your gullet. At least that's the theory. But sometimes it goes down the wrong way, and you end up choking – it's got into your windpipe, the tube you use for breathing. Instead, in movies, you often see restaurant diners leaping up and grabbing a choking person from behind to give them the "Heimlich Maneuver." These violent abdominal thrusts are meant to dislodge the blockage, but don't actually do it—experts work out how

FUNGI FLAVOR

Fungi's main role in nature is to help to rot organic matter, which is a very mucky, smelly job. Despite this, fungi is also a favorite human food. Several different types of mushrooms are used in cooking, while fungi in the form of yeast is also used for fermenting wine and beer, and for making bread.

MOLDY ILLNESS

Mold is microscopic fungi that reproduces through spores and can cause ill health. Mold colonies grow on all types of dead organic matter, including food, and in damp conditions. Some molds are used in the creation of medicines, including penicillin, but they also produce toxins which are very harmful to humans. Stachybotrys atra is believed to have caused life-threatening respiratory problems in adults and led to several infant deaths.

HUMUNGOUS FUNGUS

The largest organism in the world is a huge, revolting fungus discovered in North America. The honey mushroom Armillaria ostoyae covers 8.9sq km (3.4sq m) of the floor of the Malheur National Forest in Oregon. The fungus carpets the floor with black shoestrings and can kill some species of tree, including the Douglas fir. It is estimated that the Oregon fungus is 2,400 years old.

DOG VOMIT MOLD

Slime mold is a slippery, oozing amoeba that grows on damp, dead plant matter in forests, and sometimes reaches several metres wide. One type of this mold looks so repulsive that it is known as "dog's vomit." It is bright yellow and white, and looks as if someone has been sick after eating scrambled eggs.

FUNGUS FOOT

Many revolting human skin conditions involve fungi. Athlete's foot is an infection caused by the fungus Trichophyton, which leads to flaking, scaling, itchy skin. The fungal infection spreads through contact in swimming pools, showers, and saunas. Fungi also cause nail infections and ringworm. About a quarter of all people suffer from a fungi-related skin infection at some time in their lives.

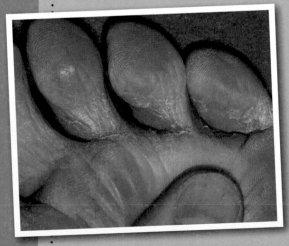

TRUFFLE HOGS

You might be eating pig's saliva when you eat a truffle. Truffles are a type of edible fungi that is unearthed by grunting, snuffling pigs. They have become one of the most highly esteemed ingredients in first-class cuisine as they have an extremely strong earthy flavor. The truffles grow underground near the base of trees. Pigs known as truffle hogs are specially trained to sniff out the fungi, digging them up from the earth with their snouts and slobbering all over them before they are sent to the best restaurants.

FROG KILLER

During 1993, frogs and salamanders in Queensland, Australia mysteriously started dying in massive numbers and no one could understand why. Then scientists discovered that it was due to a toxic fungus called Batrachochytrium dendrobatidis. This fungus has a nasty habit: it grows beneath the skin in cysts which then become so full they burst, killing the host frog, toad or salamander and infecting the watery environment around so others pick up the fungus in a horribly repeating cycle.

THE DEATH CAP

Many mushrooms, which are the fleshy fruit of fungi, are highly poisonous. Unfortunately, some of the poisonous ones look almost identical to the edible ones. The most toxic of all is the death cap mushroom, which is responsible for 90% of human deaths through eating fungi. It tastes pleasant at first, but quite soon after eating it people get a runny stomach, vomiting, and tummy pain. If untreated, the internal organs can be badly damaged, causing a terrible death a week or so later from liver failure, which causes massive toxin damage throughout the body. Just 30g (1oz) can kill an adult, and famous victims include Claudius, Emperor of Rome and the Holy Roman Emperor Charles VI.

WOW!
OVER 200 TYPES OF CARNIVOROUS FUNGI EAT TINY ROUNDWORMS.

POINTY HEADS

In 15th-century Germany, women's hats were so tall and pointed they looked like steeples on their heads. This made it difficult to walk through doors or turn the head too quickly. All hair was meant to be covered by the hats, so women also went through a gruesome process of plucking or shaving the hair from the top of their heads in the name of beauty.

KILLER CORSETS

Corsets are probably the most gruesome item of clothing ever designed. They were worn to squeeze the waist into tiny, fashionable sizes. But they also compressed the chest and ribcage area, making it hard to breathe, and squished the liver and intestines out of shape so they could not work properly. In 1859, a Frenchwoman's corset was laced so tight it snapped 3 of her lower ribs. The sharp broken bones then pierced her liver and she died.

FART-PROOFING

One U.S. company makes underpants that allow you to fart without feeling embarrassed about the whiff. They have a triangular "exit hole" with a layered carbon filter at the back. All the gas is pushed through this exit and emerges a little while later miraculously pong-free.

BIG LIPS

To make themselves more beautiful, Mursi tribeswomen from Ethiopia insert clay or wooden plates as big as saucers into their lower lips. When girls are about 15 years old, their lower lip is cut and over the next few months is plugged with larger and larger plates. This gradually stretches their lips to an incredible size – sometimes over 12cm (5in) across.

GiRAFFe NeCKS

Kayan tribal women from Burma and Thailand wear tall stacks of ornamental neck rings, which make their necks look unnaturally long. The rings are actually coils of brass which are wound round the neck so they press heavily down on the collarbones, changing their shape. The rings take hours to wind round the neck, and can be uncomfortable to wear, rubbing and discoloring skin. But once on, they are rarely taken off.

MUD MASKS

At festival time, the Asaro Mudmen of Papua New Guinea wear enormous white masks in the shape of animals' faces. They're made from clay, baked hard on to a cloth and wood frame and often have horns, teeth, ears, and gruesomely frightening expressions. The Mudmen also paint their bodies with white mud to complete the scary look – then stamp around with long bows striking fear into their enemies.

COLOR PURPLE

In ancient Rome, purple was thought to be the most aristocratic color and was worn by emperors and consuls. Purple dye, known as Tyrian Purple, was extracted from the mucus in the glands of rotting sea snails – not a job for the fainthearted! It took the mucus of 12,000 snails to produce enough dye to color a single toga, which explains why it was so amazingly expensive.

HiGHeR BeINGS

Chopines were enormously high platform-soled shoes worn by Venetian women from 1400 to 1700. The higher they were, the richer and more important the wearer – sometimes ladies tottered along on shoes a staggering 50cm (20in) tall. Chopines were made of wood so were very heavy, and injuries were common. To avoid spraining an ankle or breaking their necks, wearers had to clutch on to helpers whenever they were on the move.

10 MILLION DEAD

The Aztecs lived in the region now known as the Valley of Mexico from about 1200 to 1600. In the 16th century, almost 10 million of them were wiped out, leaving just 1 million alive. The deaths were caused by war with the Europeans and by diseases, including measles and smallpox, which the foreigners brought with them.

TASTY!

HUMAN SACRIFICE

As part of their religious ceremonies, the Aztecs used to sacrifice humans to their gods. When the Great Temple in the city of Tenochtitlán was finished in 1487, 20,000 prisoners were sacrificed as part of a special ceremony.

DOG-EATERS

The Aztec diet was very healthy, including vegetables, fruit, maize, and a lot of beans. They also loved drinking chocolate. However, some of the things they ate do not sound so pleasant, including green algae from the top of a lake as well as small dogs which were bred solely for eating.

SKULL MASK

In religious festivals, the Aztecs used to wear masks made from real human skulls. For a mask representing the god Tezcatlipoca, the back of a skull was cut away and the front was lined with deerskin, on to which a movable jaw, which still had the original owner's teeth, was hinged. The frightening skull was covered with a mosaic of semi-precious jewels, including turquoise.

CAPTIVES KILLED

Thousands of captured enemy soldiers were kept prisoner until they were needed for a sacrificial ceremony, when they would be taken to the Sacred Precinct of Tenochtitlán. Each year, captives were sacrificed to Xipe Totex, the god of fertility, and sometimes even babies were sacrificed to Tlaloc, the god of rain. The Aztecs thought the babies' tears would bring rainfall.

STONED RULER

Moctezuma II was stoned to death by his own people. He was the most famous Aztec ruler, and was so powerful that he thought he was related to the Gods. He was a great warrior but he made the mistake of welcoming the Spaniard Hernán Cortés into his capital city, Tenochtitlán. Cortés imprisoned Moctezuma and took over the city. During a riot, the Aztecs took out their anger on Moctezuma, showering him with rocks and vicious darts.

END OF THE WORLD

At the beginning of the 16th century, Aztec astronomers saw a comet in the sky and thought that it meant that their world was coming to an end. They were right. In 1519, the fearsome Hernán Cortés, a Spanish soldier, arrived in Mexico and decided to take over Tenochtitlán, despite the Aztecs welcoming him as a guest. By 1525, Spain had conquered the whole Aztec Empire.

FIERCE FIGHTERS

Dressed in animal skins and feathers, Aztec soldiers rode horses and were armed with wooden clubs with razor-sharp edges, which they would use to bash the skulls of their enemies. The Aztecs were the best soldiers in Central America, and the Aztec Empire extended its power by a combination of trade, military conquests, and marriage alliances. The political clout of the empire reached as far south as Chiapas and Guatemala

SOCIAL CONTROL

The Aztec rulers had very tight control over ordinary citizens, and would punish them very severely if they did anything wrong. If they broke the law once, they would be beaten or stabbed with sharp cactus spines.

BED OF NAILS

Hindu holy men often meditate for a few hours on a bed of nails. But that's nothing. In 1986, Ken Owen from Wales spent an incredible 300 hours (that's 12 and a half days!) lying on a bed of 600 very sharp 15cm (6in) nails. Mr. Owen says it's mind over matter, though you have to move regularly to stop the nails digging into your skin.

WOW!
US MAGICIAN DOROTHY DIETRICH IS THE ONLY WOMAN TO CATCH A BULLET BETWEEN HER TEETH!

FISH MAN

Norwegian Ronny Frimann turned into a fish man when he spent 100 hours – that's over 4 days – underwater in 2007 to raise money for charity. He wore a diving drysuit and helmet, was fed and watered through tubes and had to wee through a catheter, another tube. This was the longest any human being had been submerged underwater, and during his stunt he lost over 7kg (1st 1lb) in weight.

WHAT LUXURY?

Giovanni d'Andrea was the most famous lawyer in 14th-century Italy but he had a very strange habit. For 20 years, he slept every night on the open ground with only a bearskin to cover him, as a way of abstaining from luxurious living.

EAR'S THE BUS!

Moving a bus with your bare hands is no easy matter, but strongman Manjit Singh, known as the Iron Man of Leicester, managed to pull one using just his ears! He attached cables from his lugs to the bus with clamps, and pulled it a mighty 6.1m (20ft). He's also pulled a bus with his teeth and ponytail, which must have hurt!

FROZEN IN TIME

In 2000, wearing ordinary clothes, and shivering even before he started, US endurance artist David Blaine was encased in massive, see-through ice blocks – and stayed there for the next 63 hours 42 minutes and 15 seconds. His wee was extracted through one tube, and he was supplied with air and water through others, but he didn't eat the whole time. He was eventually cut out of the ice in New York City's Times Square with chainsaws and warmed up in hospital, though it was a month before he could walk again.

WITHOUT A PARACHUTE

In 1972, Serbian flight attendant Vesna Vulovic fell 10,600m (33,330ft) without a parachute – and lived to tell the tale. The plane she was on blew up over the Czech Republic and she landed amongst the remains of the fuselage, the only survivor. She broke her legs, fractured her skull and was temporarily paralyzed from the waist down. But she soon recovered and started flying again.

SWIM FREEZE

American Lynne Cox has a talent for swimming in water that is cold enough to kill most humans within minutes. In 1987, she swam the Bering Strait from Alaska to the Soviet Union in waters of 4ºC (40ºF) – water freezes at 0ºC (32ºF). Wearing only a swimsuit, cap, and goggles, she swam 1.9km (1.2 miles) in the waters off Antarctica in 2002. Somehow, with her head out of the water, she maintained a high enough core body temperature through the 25-minute ordeal to keep her heart beating steadily.

LIFE ON PILLAR

In the 5th century AD, Simeon Stylites spent 39 years of his life on top of a pillar. His first perch was about 4m (13ft) from the ground, though he later moved to a platform said to be 15m (49ft) high. He spent most of his time praying and barely ate anything, though local children would bring him bread and cheese from time to time. He used to drop his excrement over the side of the pillar.

MONKEY HANGERS

During the Napoleonic wars between England and France in the early 19th century, a French ship was wrecked off the coast of Hartlepool in northeast England. All the crew died, except for a monkey which was dressed in a French military uniform. The local people, who had never seen a Frenchman before, decided that the monkey was a French spy and hanged it.

ACE OF SPIES

Sydney Reilly is known as the Ace of Spies and the Real James Bond. Unlike Bond, he was captured by the Russians, tortured, taken to a dark forest, and executed. He was spying right up until his death in 1925, writing tiny notes on cigarette papers and hiding them in the plasterwork of his cell. Before he became a spy for the British, he worked as a con-man selling fake medical cures, and is believed to have committed a ruthless murder.

UMBRELLA TIP MURDER

One of the most famous assassinations by an undercover agent happened on the streets of London in 1978. Georgi Markov, a writer, had upset the Communist government in Bulgaria while he was living in Britain, and the Bulgarians decided to get rid of him. He was standing at a bus stop when a man poked his leg with the end of an umbrella. Later on, Markov saw a small red bump on his calf. The tip of the umbrella had been filled with deadly poison. After 3 days of fever and incredible pain, Markov died.

CROSS-DRESSING SPY

The South African Fritz Duquesne was an intrepid fraudster, master of disguise, and spy for the Germans, who was imprisoned in New York in 1917. In 1919 he pretended to be paralyzed and was sent to Bellevue Hospital, where he escaped dressed as a woman. In World War II, he set up an advanced spy ring to give military information to the Germans, but was discovered by J. Edgar Hoover's FBI. He was imprisoned again, and this time did not escape.

THE FIRST SPYMASTER

Francis Walsingham was the cruel, devious spymaster for Queen Elizabeth I of England in the 16th century. He was responsible for hundreds of people getting their heads chopped off. Walsingham set up an international network of undercover spies so he could find out what Queen Elizabeth's enemies were doing. He then tortured them on the bone-wrenching rack, and had many of them beheaded.

EXOTIC DANCER

No one was really sure who the most famous spy in history was working for, but she was still executed by firing squad. Mata Hari was a beautiful exotic dancer who seduced many important politicians and military officers during World War I. She was probably a double agent working for the French as well as their enemies, the Germans. Before the French shot her, she blew a kiss at the firing squad. Her head was cut off, embalmed, and sent to a museum, but it mysteriously disappeared.

NINJA HITMEN

The ninjas were merciless killers in feudal Japan from the 15th century onwards. They were spies and assassins who were specially trained in disguise, martial arts, weapons, explosives, and poisons. Warlords would send them, often solo, on covert missions to murder or sabotage their rivals. They would disguise themselves as monks, entertainers, fortune-tellers, and merchants in order to get close to their targets. Then they'd assassinate them in cold blood, using swords, daggers, darts, sickles and chains, spikes, rocket-propelled arrows, hand-held bombs, extending spears, or vicious star-shaped discs that they threw like frisbees.

AMERICA'S EARLIEST SPY

Nathan Hale was America's first spy. During the American Revolution, he volunteered to gather intelligence to use against the British. He pretended to be a Dutch teacher and went to the British stronghold of New York, but the British discovered that he was a spy and hanged him in 1776. Before his execution he said, "I only regret that I have but one life to lose for my country."

HOWLING WOLVES

Werewolves are mythical beasts, part-human, part-wolf, and are said to be able to shift their shape from one to the other during the full moon, or when they put on a wolf's skin or belt. They're strong, hairy, and ferocious, ripping apart humans to eat their flesh – and they turn whoever they bite into a werewolf, too. In France, there was a real-life werewolf mania in the 16th century. Over 30,000 people were condemned as werewolves, many were punished and some were even burnt at the stake.

THE FIRST VAMPIRE

Peter Plogojowitz was a Serbian peasant believed by his village to have become a vampire. Within 8 days of his death, 9 other local people had also died, claiming on their deathbeds that Peter had come in the night to throttle them. The locals were so fearful that they dug up his body and are said to have found it undecomposed, with new skin and nails, and fresh blood around the mouth – all taken as signs that he was indeed a vampire. A stake was driven through his heart and his body was burned.

BEAUTIFUL BLOODSUCKER

The supernatural Penanggalan of Southeast Asia looks like a beautiful woman by day. But at night she's said to detach her head from her body and fly around with her intestines dangling like a jellyfish, searching for new blood!

FLYING FLAMES

The mythical Loogaroo is a Caribbean vampire-like figure, said to be in league with the devil. By day she apparently looks like a sweet little old lady, but at night she sheds her skin and leaves it under a tree, while she flies around in a flaming blue ball of fire looking for new victims. It's said that if you hide her skin, she'll never be able to change back into human form again.

FEARSOME ZOMBIES

The Jiang shi (meaning "stiff corpse") are mythical zombie-like figures in China. They're said to have green skin, white hair, black tongues, and eyeballs which hang out of their sockets.

COUNT DRACULA

The most famous bloodsucker is found in Bram Stoker's novel, *Dracula*. Dracula is a Transylvanian count and vampire who cannot abide daylight or garlic, has to sleep on soil brought from his homeland, and can only be killed by a stake through the heart. His character was inspired by real-life baddies Vlad the Impaler, who got rid of his enemies by impaling them on sharp sticks, and Elizabeth Bathory of Transylvania, who is said to have bathed in human blood to stay young.

VOODOO MONSTERS

Zombies are said to be the living dead, people brought back from the grave and enslaved in a trance-like state through voodoo – a religion of Haiti and the Caribbean. These relentless, flesh-eating corpses are said to shuffle around in hordes, their rotting skin hanging from their bones, oblivious to injury or pain – and anyone bitten by one turns into a zombie too.

FLYSPECK

Flyspeck is fly sick or poop – and it can help show if a body has been moved. At a murder scene, flies feed on human blood, and regurgitate it around the body. If the body is then moved to another place, forensics can match the dead person's DNA to that contained in the original flyspecks – and prove the murder happened there.

BOG MUMMIES

The time a body takes to decompose depends on where it is. A body left in the open air will decay twice as fast as one under water, and four times as fast as one that has been buried underground. Bodies which end up in peat bogs, glaciers, or desert sand will stay preserved for thousands of years – the "Bog Mummy" effect. Bog Mummies' skin and internal organs are usually intact, and scientists can even find out what they ate for their last dinner.

HUMAN TRACES

DNA is short for deoxyribonucleic acid, an individual blueprint we all carry around in every cell in our body. Wherever we go, we leave traces of our DNA – from a sweaty hand, a chewed pencil, a strand of hair, even sneeze droplets or flaked-off skin cells. This is bad news for criminals. Today, scientists can take samples from crime scenes and match the DNA of suspects to it, proving them innocent – or guilty.

FINGERPRINTS

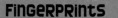

Every person's fingerprints are different, even those of identical twins, so they are a good way of telling people apart. At a crime scene, people often leave "invisible" fingerprints in natural oil or sweat, or in soft materials such as dust or wax. These can be "lifted" and identified to help catch the person who committed the crime. Some criminals go to great lengths to change their fingerprints and avoid capture – they burn or put acid on them, or have them surgically altered. In 2007, a doctor was imprisoned for replacing the fingerprints of a criminal with skin from the soles of his feet.

HUNT THE CRIMINAL

Forensics uses lots of different ways to look at the evidence left at a crime scene, to solve the crime and catch the criminals. Forensic scientists examine fingerprints, hair, and fibers, DNA from blood or saliva, tire- or footprints, and guns.

WOW! 80% OF UNKNOWN BODIES CAN BE IDENTIFIED BY THEIR TEETH.

TOOTH STORY

Skeletons, decomposed, burned, and bomb-blasted bodies can all be identified by their teeth. Tooth enamel is harder and longer-lasting than bone, and even very hot temperatures don't destroy it. Teeth are extremely individual too: legend has it that William the Conqueror, who had very crooked teeth, used a sealing wax imprinted with his bite mark so people would know his letters were really from him.

BODY FARM

At the Body Farm in Tennessee, around 50 dead bodies are lounging around in different stages of decay – some in cars, others buried in woodland, others just sitting out in the sun. This is not a gruesome movie, but part of the University of Tennessee in Knoxville, the place where scientists come to study exactly how bodies decompose.

INSECTS CAN TALK...

Some insects feed on dead bodies, which is very helpful for scientists in estimating when a person died. The first insects to arrive on a body are blow flies, which lay eggs that turn into maggots. The number and location of maggots and flies can help pinpoint the time of death. Hide beetles prefer tough tendons and bones, and arrive later in a body's decomposition.

BANNED PONG

The durian is probably the strangest fruit in the world. It's hard to get into and it absolutely stinks. The fruit is very ugly, with a tough, thick, thorn-covered skin. If you manage to get into one, you will wonder why you went to all that effort because you will be immediately hit with a gut-wrenching, gag-inducing stench. Its creamy flesh tastes like almond custard and is loved by many Southeast Asian people. However, its smell has led it to being banned on public transport.

ALIEN FINGERS

The fruit called Buddha's hand does not really look like the hand of the Buddha. It looks like part of a grotesque alien. Also known as the fingered citron, the fruit has peculiar, wrinkled, curled yellow tentacles that are horrible to touch. There is hardly any flesh inside the fingers, but it is very fragrant so the fruit is used to perfume rooms in Asia.

DIRTY STICK FOOD

Goatsbeard looks like a horrible, dirty stick which you would never dream of eating. It also has nasty little entrails sticking out of the end, which is where it gets its name from. In fact, goatsbeard looks like a stick because it is the root of the purple salsify plant. It tastes a little bit like oysters. In many countries, the salsify plant is treated like an unwanted weed.

UGLY UGLI

The ugli fruit really is an ugly fruit. It looks battered, bruised, and moldy, with rough and wrinkled skin, even when it is fresh and in perfect condition. The ugli, which originally comes from Jamaica in the Caribbean, is a very strange hybrid. It is made by cross-fertilizing 3 other fruit – the orange, grapefruit, and tangerine – but it doesn't look as tasty as any of them. It tastes like a sour orange.

ALIEN FUNGUS!!

BIZARRE BROCCOLI

Another food that looks like it has come from a different planet is Romanesco broccoli. It is related to the cauliflower, but its bright green florets grow in individual, spiral-shaped lumps which make it look like a kind of freaky fungus or creepy coral which could have come from outer space.

SLIMY DINOSAUR EGG

The African horned melon looks like a prehistoric dinosaur egg, but it is even more peculiar when you open it up. The bright orange skin is covered with spiky horns, and the inside looks like green slime that is full of seeds.

LAXATIVE DRAGON

The pitaya, also known as dragon's fruit, is a very peculiar pink fruit with horrifying green tongues sticking out from it. It has white flesh and black seeds inside, but one type has disturbing blood-red flesh. The sour fruit tastes refreshing but it is also used as a laxative. If you eat too much dragon's fruit, you will spend the rest of the day on the toilet.

SWEET AND SOUR MIRACLE

Miracle fruit doesn't look very strange, but it does something so weird that it makes you think that you have gone crazy. If you eat just one small red berry, it will completely change the way some things taste. Sharp, citrus lemon will suddenly taste like candy, while acidic vinegar and pickles will taste like sweet apple. The sensation is so strange that people eat miracle fruit at special flavor-tripping parties.

SOAP MISER

Henrietta Green, who lived in New York, was incredibly rich but she was also a horrible stinker. In 1864, when she was 30, she inherited $7.5 million from her father, but she was too mean to buy any new clothes and wore the same disgustingly dirty black dress until it wore out. She hardly ever washed, and when she did, she never used hot water or soap.

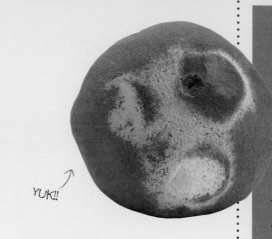

YUK!!

NO WASHING-UP

Medieval people were not very fond of washing-up. Most people would walk around with their own sharp knife, which they would use for all sorts of purposes, and a spoon, which they would get out at meal times. Food was served on stale bread rather than a plate. At the end of the meal, they would usually just wipe the knife and lick the spoon clean.

SMELLY SAXONS

Despite previous centuries of Roman rule, when regular bathing was normal, the Saxons of the Dark Ages seem to have had no idea about personal hygiene. Even monks used to have a bath only a couple of times a year. They were covered with fleas and lice, and often used to eat food which was dirty or moldy.

WALLS OF DUNG

Animal dung was often used to build peasants' homes. The walls would be made from "wattle and daub." Thin branches of wood were woven together and covered with a mixture of mud, straw, and dung, which would dry and become hard.

BED BUGS

Beds were very stinky during the medieval era and were often covered with bugs. Some people would sprinkle their straw mattresses with strong-smelling herbs including lavender, tansy, and lady's bedstraw. The herbs would cover the bad smells and also put off fleas. Most peasants did not bother with herbs, though, and would be covered with itchy bites.

STINKY CLOTHES

In the medieval era, the more hygienic peasants would sometimes change their underwear (but nowhere near as often as we do today), but they would wear the same outer garments for months and months. Luckily, most people smelt of wood-smoke from their fires, which would cover up the ghastly smell.

VILE VIKINGS

Surprisingly, the hairy, war-mongering Vikings had soap. They made it out of horse chestnuts. The Vikings had long hair, which their wives would comb to get rid of the nits. They were still very smelly, though, spending months on their boats without washing.

KING OF STENCH

It was not just peasants who were smelly. In the 16th century, Henry IV, King of France from 1589 to 1610, was famous for dodging soap. He would not wash even after going hunting. His mistress once told him that he smelt like a dead animal. The first time she met him, his future wife Marie de Medici fainted because of his stench. King Louis XIV of France also hated water and is believed to have had only a couple of baths in his entire life.

HYGIENE HORRORS

Unfortunately, we know exactly what a stinker Samuel Pepys was because he kept a famous diary and hardly ever mentioned washing. The 17th-century Englishman did not seem to like going near a bath. When he did wash, it was because his wife made him. On one occasion, he thought that he had become ill because he had washed his feet the night before.

BLiSTeR BeeTLe

You can probably guess how this horrible insect gets its name! When it is attacked, it emits a disgusting secretion called Canthardin, which causes blisters to appear all over people's skin. Cantharidin is a poisonous, highly toxic chemical that is actually used in medicine to remove warts.

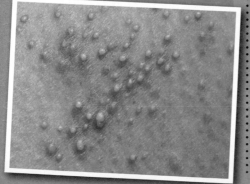

AnT SLAYeRS

Dorylus ants may be very, very small, but they look frightening when there are 50 million of them marching in a column. The huge columns kill anything in their way, using their very strong jaws to give animals multiple, painful bites. Even humans have been killed by them, but usually by asphyxiation, as they stop breathing when millions of ants swarm over them. At mating time, males have their wings ripped off and they are made to mate with the queen ant before they die.

BUG HOUSeS

Termites eat wood, rather than soft leaves, which give them the strength to be the world's most amazing builders. They can build a huge mound out of just dirt, dung, and their own saliva. Some mounds in Africa are 9m (30ft) high. Termites may be good at building their own houses, but they are also good at destroying human homes. About 50 houses in the U.S. are destroyed every year because of termites eating the wood and causing structural damage.

CARCASS HOme

When a burying beetle finds a rotting animal carcass, it attracts a mate to help bury it and together they use it as a house for their young. They burrow a pit in the carcass and then the larvae live in the pit. If the adults think that the carcass is not big enough to feed the whole family, they will kill some of the young.

UGH!
THE BOMBARDIER BEETLE PELTS ENEMIES WITH A BOILING, FOUL-SMELLING LIQUID.

DUNG EATER

Dung beetles feed almost entirely on excrement. There are 3 main types. The most famous are called rollers, which roll dung into a huge ball, sometimes up to 50 times their own weight. Rollers often have to fight other dung beetles who want their ball. Other types of dung beetles are tunnelers, which bury the dung where they find it, and dwellers, who just live in it. The beetles feed by squeezing the juice out of the manure.

INDESTRUCTIBLE ROACH

The cockroach is as indestructible as it is disgusting. They are scuttling, flying, horrible household pests which are extremely hard to exterminate. They can live without food or water for up to 3 months and survive freezing temperatures, total water immersion, and even a whack from a shoe. Unbelievably, you can chop off a cockroach's head and it could still scuttle around your house for a week before dying of thirst because its brain is not in its head, but scattered throughout its body. Yuk!

OMEN OF DEATH

The deathwatch beetle is thought to be an omen of impending death. It lives in old wood, including the rafters of very old houses. On quiet nights, including during vigils at the bedside of the sick or dying, the ticking noise the beetle makes to attract mates can often be heard. As a result, it is known as the "deathwatch" beetle.

BiG SHOt

Walter Hudson was one of the world's fattest men. He weighed around 544kg (1,200lb) and had a waist span of more than 3m (119in). He shot to fame in 1987 when he got stuck in his bathroom door and had to be rescued by the local fire department – it's said to have taken 9 men to carry him back to bed. When he died in 1991 aged 46, rescue workers had to cut a big hole in his bedroom wall because he couldn't fit through the door, and a forklift was used to move his body.

COUCH POTAtO

When she broke her leg, Gayle Laverne Grinds sat on the same couch without moving for the next 6 years! By the time rescue workers were called to help her, she weighed 217kg (476lb) and ate and slept on her makeshift bed – she was too big even to get up and go to the bathroom. She had to be carried to hospital on the couch. Doctors couldn't dislodge her and she died while still attached to it.

LiFt AND FOLD

Strange things are often found in the fat folds of the very overweight. Pens, rubbers, household objects, bits of food – it's even been known for whole sandwiches to turn up, usually when people are being washed by helpers. But the most astonishing items were hidden by George Vera. When this 227kg (500lb) man was arrested in Texas, U.S.A., he was searched 5 times but somehow managed to hide a 9mm handgun and two clips deep in his fat folds. He finally told police about the gun 2 days later and they confiscated it.

THRiFtY GeNeS

Around 300 million people in the world are clinically obese. Most live in the U.S.A., Canada, the Middle East, UK, Australasia, and the Pacific Islands. On the island of Nauru, about 80% of adults are obese. But obesity doesn't just occur in rich countries – in many developing nations, rates are soaring. In some Chinese cities, as many as 20% of people are now obese. It's thought this is caused by "thrifty metabolism" – people who have been used to living without much food for generations process it very efficiently. But when food becomes abundant, their bodies store it as massive wodges of fat.

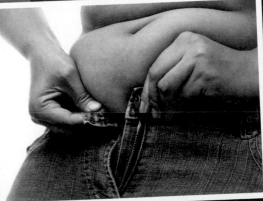

SUPERSIZE SURGERY

Some very fat people try surgery to help them lose weight. Sometimes a band is tied around their stomach to make it smaller, and to make them feel fuller so they eat less. Other people have their fat removed by liposuction. In this operation, a hollow tube is inserted under the skin and sucks out the yellow fat which lies there. Sometimes 4kg (8lb) of fat is removed in a single treatment – that's the same as 4 large bags of sugar.

WOW! A SIAMESE CAT IN RUSSIA WEIGHED AN ASTONISHING 23KG (50LB) – THE AVERAGE WEIGHT OF A 7-YEAR-OLD GIRL!

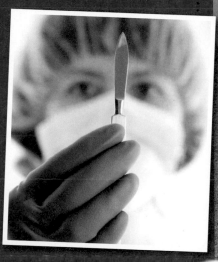

AIMING HIGH

New Jersey native Donna Simpson wants to become the world's fattest woman. She currently weighs around 273kg (602lb or 43st) and is eating a whopping 12,000 calories a day, 6 times more than the recommended daily intake for women, to reach her dream weight of 450kg (1,000lb or 71st).

AVALANCHE FREEZE
The Wellington Avalanche in February 1910 was the worst in the history of the United States. The town was hit by an appalling 9-day blizzard, with 3.4m (11ft) of snow falling in just 1 day. A 3m (10ft) wall of snow from the mountain headed towards Wellington, hit 2 trains in the depot at 1am one night, throwing the trains 46m (150ft) downhill and killing 96 passengers who were asleep. Their corpses lay there for 21 weeks, because the weather prevented their earlier retrieval.

MULTIPLE TORNADO TERROR
Super Outbreak of 1974, the largest of multiple tornados in Canada and the U.S.A., killed over 300 people. It consisted of an incredible 148 tornadoes happening over 18 hours – 16 raging at one time. They lifted roofs, railroad cars, and churches, sucked a lady's shoes as she clung desperately to a man's hands, and hurled cows into the air.

IT'S POURING FROGS

Sometimes people are pelted with fish, frogs or birds raining down on them. Witnesses of this rare event describe the animals as being startled, though normally healthy! In other instances, they come down as yucky carcasses frozen to death or encased in ice. The phenomenon is believed to be caused when strong winds traveling over water pick up the frogs, birds or toads, and carry them several miles inland.

CYCLONE BAY
The Bhola Cyclone hit East Pakistan and India's West Bengal in 1970. With winds reaching 185kph (115mph), the cyclone took up to 500,000 lives. Survivors were left with "Cyclone Syndrome" – severe abrasions on their limbs and chest caused by clinging to trees.

YUK!
IN 1894, A SHOWER OF JELLYFISH FELL ON THE CITY OF BATH IN ENGLAND!

BLOOD RAIN

Sometimes a red-colored rainwater falls which people call "rains of blood" – most recently in Southern India in 2001.

No one knows exactly what causes this spooky occurrence, though there are many theories. The wackiest theory is that tiny alien organisms have been carried to Earth by a comet or meteor from outer space. But it's more likely to be tiny particles of red clay from sand storms or rock dust from erupting volcanoes!

FISH FALL

Every year, it rains fish in Honduras! This unusual weather event has been going on for over 100 years – there's even an annual festival called the "Lluvia de Peces" ("Rain of Fishes"). Every summer, the sky darkens terribly, there's a lightning storm and heavy rain pelts down for a couple of hours. Afterwards, slimy, half-dead fish are found flapping and gasping all over the ground – often people take them home, and cook and eat them! Some of the fish are blind, and one theory is they're flooded out from subterranean rivers and caught up by the wind in the terrible violence of the storm.

BALL LIGHTNING

Slow-moving balls of lightning are sometimes seen floating in the sky and even inside buildings during or after thunderstorms. Sometimes they can be lethal. In 1753, scientist Georg Richmann tried to "capture" ball lightning in an experiment, but the glowing sphere exploded on his forehead – his clothes were fried by the high voltage, his shoes were blown from his feet, the door was torn from its hinges, and the doorframe was split in half. Needless to say, he died instantly. Ball lightning lasts for around 25 seconds, and is white, orange or blue. Nobody knows what causes it but over 10,000 cases have been recorded!

SHAPE SHIFTING

Witches were thought to be able to "shape shift" or turn themselves into animals so they could run around the countryside with the devil. In 1662, young Scottish witch Isobel Gowdie confessed that she and her coven (group of witches) often transformed themselves into hares by repeating three times: "I shall go into a hare, With sorrow and sych and meickle care; And I shall go in the Devil's name, Ay while I come home again."

DEVIL'S MARKS

Any wart, protuberance, strange birthmark or mole could have you accused of being a witch. But the most obvious sign was an extra nipple on the chest or abdomen. This was thought to be where the witch's familiar – a spirit helper in the form of a cat or dog – suckled.

FIRST WITCH?

One of the first witches was Circe, who appeared in Homer's epic poem *The Odyssey*. She drugged Odysseus's friends then turned them into pigs with her wand. When she tried to trap Odysseus with a magical potion, he was clever enough to refuse it, and managed to escape and free his men from her curse.

SPELLBOUND

Anne Boleyn had a fifth finger on one hand – which many people believed was the sure sign of a witch. When Henry VIII tired of her because she could not produce a male heir, he said she'd won his love by laying spells on him. Her witchy reputation then made it easier for him to have her beheaded.

WITCH CAKES

During the Salem witch trials in Massachusetts, "witch cakes" were made using rye and the wee of the accused witch and fed to a dog. If the dog started behaving strangely, or the woman was in pain while the dog ate the cake, then she was instantly declared to be a witch.

WOW!

THE LAST WITCH WAS BURNED IN ENGLAND IN 1712.

WEIGHTY MATTERS

In Oudewater in the Netherlands, the Weighing House was a place where people accused of witchcraft could prove their innocence. People believed that witches had no souls and weighed much less than normal people – which is why they could fly around on broomsticks. If they hit a certain weight on the Heksenwaag or witches' scales, then they were innocent and given a certificate to prove it.

WHAT WIZARDRY!

Male wizards and warlocks have been around since the story of Merlin, but John Dee was one of the most extraordinary. He was a magician, mathematician, and astrologer at the court of Elizabeth I who studied sorcery and claimed to be in touch with angels. He used a crystal ball to contact them while they apparently taught him magic spells and even, he said, dictated several books to him.

WITCH MANIA

People thought witches were in league with the devil, and during the 16th and 17th centuries, frenzied witch-hunts broke out all over Europe and the U.S.A. Terrible tortures were inflicted on anyone suspected of sorcery, including branding, the scold's bridle – an iron headpiece – and burning at the stake. Witches were also "ducked" in ponds – if the woman sank and drowned, she was innocent. If she floated, she was guilty.

BREW-HA-HA!

A "grimoire" is a sacred spell book which contains instructions on how to cast spells, make magical objects like talismen, and call up spirits and demons. Typical spells involve boiling a cauldron full of newts' eyes, rats' tails, graveyard dust, toenail clippings, and toads' entrails – delicious!

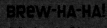

BiG FALSiES

George Washington lost most of his teeth early in life. While he was U.S. president, he had several sets of falsies, some for eating, some for talking and speech-making, and others for "ornamental" occasions such as having his portrait painted. The only complete set that still exists today is made of a mixture of ivory, human, and cow's teeth on heavy lead "gums" – surely for show days only.

PAiNFUL GRiN

People in Mexico 2,000 years ago liked to adorn their gnashers. Mayan dentists used hand drills to engrave grooves and notches on people's front teeth, then would implant jade, turquoise, and other colorful stones in each tooth. Their patients would have dazzling smiles, but all that drilling must have hurt!

EEK! DEKE SLAYTON, PILOT ON THE APOLLO-SOYUZ, LOST A FINGER TO A MOWER AS A BOY.

FiRSt FOOt

Egyptian embalmers often added false limbs to mummies, so bodies which had been maimed in life would be restored for the afterlife. The mummy of one 14-year-old Egyptian girl was found with two false legs attached, with her feet made out of reeds and mud. Another Egyptian noblewoman had a beautifully carved false toe, made of wood and leather.

HALF MAN

Talk about unlucky – by the age of 25, Spanish admiral Blas de Lezo had lost so many body parts in battle that people called him "Mediohombre" or "half man." First he was spattered with cannon shot in the left leg and had to have it amputated, then he lost his left eye, then his right arm was chopped off in the Siege of Barcelona. Undeterred by all his missing body parts, he kept fighting for the next 27 years until eventually dying of plague.

IRON LEGS

When knights in the Middle Ages lost a limb, they used to get the metalworker who made their armor to run them up a new arm or leg made of iron. The false limb would be heavy to walk on, painful when fitted over the stump wound, and would have clanked so badly you'd hear the injured knight coming for miles.

FAKE LEG

CAPTAIN HOOK

Sea pirating was a dangerous profession and pirates would often lose their limbs in cutlass fights. Just like Captain Hook in *Peter Pan* or Long John Silver in *Treasure Island*, they'd wear false metal hands shaped into hooks and hollow wooden pegs for legs. There weren't any doctors around so the ship's cook often performed amputations, and the false limbs would be attached to the stumps with leather straps.

BIONIC BOTTOM

Ged Galvin from Yorkshire, UK, had his rear end rebuilt after a car accident left his insides badly damaged. Surgeons took muscle from his leg and wrapped it around his sphincter – the circular bit at the end of the rectum – then attached electrodes to the nerves to make the new muscle move. He goes to the toilet using a remote control which he carries around in his pocket like a mobile phone.

AYE, AYE, EYE!

In the 1950s, opticians' shops used to have trays of one hundred or more false eyeballs of all colors, shapes, and sizes. They were called "stock eyes," and people in need of a new eyeball could search through to find the color and fit they liked best.

NEW NOSES FOR OLD

In the olden days, people were always losing their noses in fights or because of disease. If you were rich enough, you could buy a new one to plonk over the top. Danish astronomer Tycho Brahe got his nose chopped off in a duel when he was 20, and wore a false one made of silver and gold for the rest of his life.

WOW!

MANY ACTORS THINK MACBETH HAS SPECIAL DARK POWERS AND REFUSE TO SAY HIS NAME OUT LOUD.

DEADLY ROMANCE

Romeo and Juliet is one of the most famous love stories ever told, but it is really a dark tragedy. The young lovers come from families that hate each other, so they decide to marry in secret. Disapproving of their love, Juliet's cousin Tybalt stabs Romeo's friend and in return Romeo kills Tybalt. Later, Romeo wrongly thinks that Juliet has died, so he takes poison. When Juliet finds out Romeo is dead, she stabs herself to death.

THE GORY WRITER

Shakespeare may be known as the greatest playwright in the world, famous for his use of language, but many of his plays involve some gruesome action. The English playwright lived from 1564 to 1616, which was a gory time in history, and some of his plays reflect the era, featuring intrigue, poisonings, and stabbings.

POUND OF FLESH

In *The Merchant of Venice*, a cruel money-lender called Shylock allows his enemy, the merchant Antonio, to borrow some money on the condition that, if he fails to repay the loan, Antonio must give Shylock a pound of his own flesh. When Antonio becomes bankrupt, Shylock demands the flesh, but his plan fails on a legal technicality. To this day, people say that someone acting without mercy "demands his pound of flesh."

MAD OLD KING

King Lear is a tragic play in which an old king leaves his kingdom to two of his three daughters, but soon becomes mad, thinking he has been tricked out of his kingdom. Meanwhile, in their pursuit of power, the daughters start to act madly themselves. One of them poisons her sister and then commits suicide, while the third daughter is murdered by a power-hungry nobleman. With all his daughters dead, King Lear also dies of grief.

TO BE OR NOT
TO BE

VENGEFUL PRINCE

Almost everyone dies in *Hamlet*, one of Shakespeare's most famous plays. Hamlet takes revenge on his uncle, who has poisoned his father and married his mother. He accidentally kills his girlfriend Ophelia's father and she commits suicide. Ophelia's brother challenges Hamlet to a duel and stabs him with a poisoned blade, but before he dies, Hamlet manages to kill his uncle.

MOST GRUESOME PLAY

Shakespeare's most gruesome play is *Titus Andronicus*, full of murders, amputations, and cannibalism. Titus, a Roman general, kills the eldest son of a Goth queen in revenge for the death of two of his sons. The queen's other sons then cut off the hands and tongue of Titus's daughter. Titus kills them and cooks them in a pie, which he tricks the queen into eating. By the end of the play, most of the characters have been murdered.

THE SCOTTISH MURDERER

Spurred on by three mysterious witches who prophesy that he will become king of Scotland in Shakespeare's *Macbeth*, kills King Duncan and frames some guards, whom he also kills before they can protest their innocence. He is crowned king but becomes insanely suspicious of everyone and kills the wife and children of his rival Macduff. Macduff gets his revenge, beheading Macbeth after a battle.

NASTY HISTORY

Shakespeare often used the gory history of England's rulers in his plays. In *Richard III*, the playwright reveals how an ugly hunchback gains the throne by killing his own brother and putting the young heirs to the throne in prison in the Tower of London. He then has the heirs murdered, too.

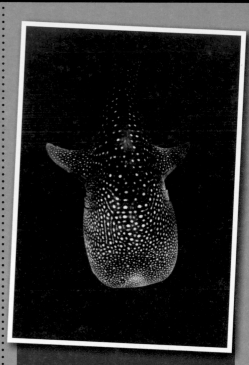

THE BIGGEST SHARK

The biggest type of shark is the huge whale shark, which can weigh up to 21,000kg (46,300lb) and can be 12.5m (40ft) long. But it is not frightening to humans or any other large animals. It mostly eats plankton, a mixture of tiny plants and animals that drift in the water. It continuously sucks in food through its huge mouth, which can be 1.5m (5ft) wide.

NEW JERSEY KILLER

The U.S.A. has had more human shark attacks than any other country in the world. In total, there have been over 1,000 recorded incidents. The most famous attacks were off the coast of New Jersey in 1916. Four bathers were killed, probably by great white sharks, in 3 separate incidents. One 14-year-old boy miraculously survived when his father and brother won a tug-of-war with a shark that bit his leg. The attacks inspired the movie *Jaws*.

GARBAGE EATER

The tiger shark is known as the "wastebasket of the sea" as it is happy to eat all types of junk as well dolphins, turtles, other species of sharks, and the occasional human. It is very aggressive and usually eats prey whole without looking at it too carefully. License plates, tires, and even baseballs have been found inside them.

HUMAN ATTACKS

Sharks may sometimes be vicious, scary creatures, but they do not usually attack humans. Only 4 species have regularly launched unprovoked human attacks: the great white, tiger, bull, and oceanic whitetip sharks. On average, only 4.3 humans die per year from unprovoked shark attacks. It is best not to provoke them, though. They are stronger and faster than any human in the water.

FLOATING PREY

The oceanic whitetip does not sound like a vicious shark, but it loves to feed on humans. The species particularly enjoyed World War II, when many ships were sunk, leaving their passengers at the mercy of the sharks. When the USS *Indianapolis* was torpedoed by the Japanese on 30 July 1945, the survivors were left floating in the water for almost 5 days. Oceanic whitetips started to attack, killing about 80 of them in the biggest human shark attack in history.

WACKY HAMMERHEAD

The weirdest looking shark is the hammerhead, which gets its name from the strange shape of its head, which is flat and very wide. This weird shape gives it extremely good vision and an excellent sense of smell, especially for blood. Some species have been known to attack humans, but mostly they eat other sharks, fish, octopus, and stingrays. Sometimes they eat their own young.

GREAT WHITE SLAYER

The great white shark, the world's largest predatory fish, is an advanced killing machine. It is fast, agile, and has a speedy, powerful bite. Luckily, it does not like the taste of humans too much. It would rather eat dolphins, sea lions, and seals, ambushing them in surprise attacks. It will sometimes tuck into the carcasses of dead whales. On average, it is 5m (16ft) long.

SPEED MASTER

If a mako shark has decided that you will be its dinner, there is little point in trying to swim away. It is the fastest shark, reaching up to 74kph (46mph) for very short bursts. It eats swordfish, tuna, and other large fish, and has been known to take a bite out of a human. It should be more scared of us, though. It has become a popular human food. The mako now needs to be protected from over-fishing.

HEAVY LEGS

Convicts used to wear leg-irons weighing about 6.4kg (14lb) to stop them running away. Sometimes they lived on old disused warships called hulks, which were really floating prisons. At night they'd sleep in the cramped, filthy hulks, and during the day would work in the dockyards wearing their heavy leg-irons 24 hours a day – so they'd sink in the water if they ever tried to escape.

RUSSIAN EXILE

From the 17th century onwards, prisoners in imperial Russia were often sent to "katorgas" in the freezing wastes of Siberia. This was a horrible exile, usually ending in death. Inmates were forced to do hard, physical labor and got beaten up at the whim of the commander. Many inmates died from disease, exhaustion and hunger – there was never enough food to go round – and prisoners were immediately killed if they attempted to make their escape.

WORLD'S WORST?

The world's most notorious prison was Carandiru Penitentiary in Brazil. Conditions were appalling – often 10 men were living in a cell meant for 2, and they saw daylight so rarely their skin turned yellow. Vicious gangs ruled over murder, corruption, torture, drugs, disease, and squalor. In 1992, open warfare broke out between guards and inmates and 102 prisoners were shot dead. Ten years later, the government decided there was only one way to get rid of Carandiru – the infamous building was razed to the ground.

SADISTIC CRANK!

In some 19th-century prisons, crank handles were installed in the cells. Convicts were told by cruel warders to turn the heavy handle 2,000 times if they wanted breakfast, and 10,000 times a day for dinner. The crank turned over a drum filled with sand, but served no other purpose. Some warders could make it harder to turn the crank by tightening a screw outside the cell – which is why prison guards are known as "screws."

ISLANDS OF INFAMY

Steep cliff faces, rocks, treacherous sea currents, and isolation make island prisons feared and notoriously hard to escape from. The most infamous was the Devil's Island Penal Colony off the coast of French Guiana. Only the most hardened thieves and criminals were sent to this disease-ridden island – 80,000 of them were said to have died there. The only escape was through tropical jungle or across the turbulent seas. One French prisoner, Henri Charrière, wrote a fictionalized account of his many attempted escapes – he floated for 3 days at sea on a sack of coconuts with his exhausted companion, who drowned in quicksand, before eventually arriving safely on the shores of the mainland.

TREADMILL

Days of hard labor and drudgery were meant to make prison life as gruesome as possible so inmates would never want to return. One common 19th-century punishment was called the "treadmill." The treadmill was a revolving paddle-wheel drum with steps or blades which the prisoner endlessly walked along to turn the wheel. It was exhausting, like lifting your legs to walk upstairs for hours on end. If a prisoner stopped, they'd fall off the wheel and injure themselves, or be beaten by prison guards. The power generated by the treadmills was often used to turn mill wheels and grind corn.

BLACK HOLE OF CALCUTTA

In 1756, 146 British prisoners-of-war and their Anglo-Indian helpers were said to be jammed into a tiny guard room in Fort William, Calcutta and left there overnight. By next morning, 123 of them had died of suffocation, heat exhaustion, thirst, trampling, or sheer terror. The room measured just 4.3m x 5.5m (14ft x 18ft), and the heat inside was intense. The prisoners were packed in so tightly that many of their corpses were said to be standing where they died.

TREE POISON!

The stinging tree, which grows in the rainforests of Indonesia, can make a person's skin come out in terrible lumps and bumps. When someone brushes up against it, the tiny, glass-sharp hairs in the leaves and fruits can become embedded in the skin. Once there, the hairs release a poison which affects the nervous system and causes incredible pain – people say it's like being hit all over their body. The pain gradually goes away but can recur, even months later.

DEATHLY BLUE

Some people have blue skin, nails and gums but they're not the Na'vi in the movie *Avatar!* Sufferers look as if they've just risen from the grave. People's skin turns blue when they have very, very high levels of silver in the body. Once that's happened, there's no going back for them. They're blue for the rest of their lives!

TREE MAN OF JAVA

Indonesian fisherman Dede Koswara's skin started producing warty, bark-like protuberances when he was 15. After a while, these grew into long, tree-like growths and he became known as the Tree Man of Java. The growths are caused by a common virus which Mr. Koswara doesn't have a good ability to fight – so it hijacked his skin cells into creating these massive warty horns. So far he's had more than 6kg (14lb) of them removed.

STRIPED SKIN

Did you know that humans have strange stripes on their skin which are normally invisible? They make a "V" shape around the back, waves on the head, and "S" shapes on the sides and front of the body. They're called Lines of Blaschko after the doctor who first noticed them, and can only be seen by the naked eye after people have contracted certain skin diseases. It's thought they trace the pathways of early cell development, when the baby was growing in the womb.

YUK! EVERY DAY YOU SHED AROUND 500 MILLION SKIN SCALES, 10 MILLION OF WHICH CARRY BACTERIA.

Queen Bee

Poppaea, the wife of Roman Emperor Nero, had a very high-maintenance skin regime. When she got up, she bathed her face and body in asses' milk. If she had a zit, she'd apply barley flour and butter paste to it, then lemon juice to bleach her freckles. Her skin would then be covered with chalk to whiten it, the delicate veins marked with blue paint, and her face painted with a white lead-based cream – which unfortunately was toxic!

Biggest Zit?

Most pimples don't grow any larger than about 5mm (⅛in). But carbuncles are a different story altogether and can grow to a whopping size. These deep, pus-filled abscesses usually occur on the back or neck, and infect lots of hair follicles at the same time. They can quickly grow to the size of a golf ball."

Acne Attack

Most zits come up one at a time. But when the deep layers of the skin get swollen and infected with acne, it's a different story. Acne is very common, almost three-quarters of teenagers get it and lots of adults, too. It happens when the skin produces too much natural oil which clogs up the small holes in which the hairs live. Acne bacteria thrive in this airless place causing redness, swelling, and pus. This pus wants to pop up to the skin surface but sometimes it's down too deep so it spreads sideways instead – eventually causing gruesome pus-filled eruptions over a large area of skin.

THE VAMPIRES

Vampire bats are legendary bloodsuckers, but in reality they lap blood up rather than suck it out. The common vampire bat, which is native to North America, feeds on humans and other mammals. It has special heat receptors which tell it where the blood of its prey flows closest to the surface of skin. The bat attacks at night, usually while its victim is sleeping, and bites into the skin with its sharp, pointy front teeth to make the blood flow.

JUMPING SUCKERS

Fleas are small, wingless insects that are the greatest jumpers in the animal kingdom. They can jump 200 times their own body length to land on mammals, including humans, in order to suck their blood. They cause very itchy bites.

↑ ITCHY!!

YUK!

MALE VAMPIRE MOTHS DRILL A FEEDING TUBE INTO HUMAN SKIN IN ORDER TO SUCK UP BLOOD.

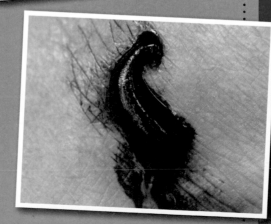

MEDICINAL SUCKER

Leeches attach themselves to an animal with a sucker, and do not let go until they are full of blood. They can consume up to 5 times their normal bodyweight in blood. While they are sucking the blood out, they produce an anesthetic so that the host animal cannot feel them on their skin.

HUMAN BLOOD BUG

The cockroach may be the most hated household bug, but the bed bug runs it a close second. Bed bugs are much smaller than cockroaches, but they are more disgusting as they feed solely on human blood. They infest bedrooms, coming out at night to feed on their human hosts by piercing their skin with two hollow feeding tubes. They can ingest up to 6 times their own body weight in blood.

HORROR KISSER

Many types of assassin bug are gruesome hunters because they kill and eat all other insects, and some of them are also called "kissing bugs" because of the way they attack humans. They bite people on the lips and around the eyes while they are sleeping and then suck out their blood. Kissing bugs live in Central and South America.

DISEASE CARRIERS

Ticks are the ultimate bloodsuckers. They can eat up to 600 times their own body size in blood. A tick inserts a cutting tool and a feeding tube into the skin of birds, reptiles, and mammals, including humans. They also transmit diseases including Lyme disease and Colorado tick fever. A mass attack of up to 30,000 ticks can cause the paralysis or death of a mammal.

LADY KILLER

Mosquitoes feed on humans and spread diseases, but the culprits are all female. The males only feed on nectar and plants, but some species of female need to have a meal of blood before they can produce eggs. While they are feeding, they transmit diseases including malaria, yellow fever, and dengue fever. This makes the female mosquito the biggest killer of humans in the world.

FORCE-FED DUCK

Foie gras, one of the most famous ingredients in French high-class cooking, is made by force-feeding a duck or goose until it virtually explodes. Foie gras means "fat liver." A funnel is pushed down the bird's throat and then a massive amount of food is poured down the tube. The bird eats so much that its liver grows to 10 times its normal size. The fatty liver is then served in fine restaurants.

MONKEY BRAINS

The revolting menu of the Manchu Han imperial feast in China a few hundred years ago included bear's paws, ape's lips, and fresh, raw monkey brains. There are stories that the monkey's brains were eaten out of its skull while it was still alive. Monkey's brains are still eaten today in some parts of Asia, but they are usually served more simply on a banana leaf.

SNAIL MANIA

Slippery, slimy snails are a specialty of French cuisine. They may be covered in oozing mucus and have two funny tentacles sticking out of their heads, but the French, who call them "escargots," love to munch on a plateful of snails. They are usually cooked in their shells with just a touch of garlic and parsley butter. The Greeks like snails, too, and buy them from the supermarket while they are still alive. The demand for snails is now so great that there are special snail farms around the world.

FATAL FISH

Chefs risk their lives when they eat fugu, the most notorious dish on the menu of top Japanese restaurants. Fugu is made from pufferfish, a type of fish which is lethally poisonous to humans. Eating it kills several people each year and puts dozens more in hospital. The fish has to be prepared very carefully to avoid using any poisonous parts, and is usually sliced extremely thinly and eaten raw. Traditionally, fugu is served on a plate decorated with a chrysanthemum flower, which in Japan is a symbol of death.

TWITCHING FROG LEGS

Slippery frog legs often twitch when they are being cooked. They are a delicacy in both French and Chinese cuisine, and are also eaten in some American states, including Louisiana and Florida. The frogs are dead when they are cooked, having been skinned and had their entrails pulled out, but the heat of cooking sometimes makes their muscles spasm so they twitch as if they are alive.

CHILI CON BARMY

One British chef likes combining very unusual ingredients. He makes bacon-and-egg ice-cream, green snail porridge, sardine-on-toast sorbet, and salty caviar and white chocolate sweets. Heston Blumenthal, who runs the famous Fat Duck restaurant in Berkshire, even concocted a pink "drink me" potion from *Alice's Adventures in Wonderland* made of cherry pie, toffee, toast, and turkey.

ROADKILL RESTAURANTS

Dead animals that have been squashed and scraped off the roads are now starting to be eaten in homes and restaurants. Chefs such as the UK's Fergus Drennan are happy to peel a fox off the highway and pot-roast it in red wine with wild mushrooms. There are now cookbooks dedicated to roadkill recipes.

FRANKENSTEIN'S MONSTER

Hideously ugly with glowing watery eyes, black lips, and thin yellow skin through which you could see his veins and muscles – this is the nameless monster first described in Mary Shelley's 1818 novel *Frankenstein*. In movie versions, the actor Boris Karloff made Frankenstein's monster look even more gruesome – he was hideously stitched and bolted together with jagged surgical scars, a Neanderthal forehead, and spooky deep-set eyes.

NASTY MUMMY

In the 1932 movie *The Mummy*, an ancient Egyptian priest Imhotep, mummified alive as punishment, is revived when an archeologist accidentally reads a life-giving spell. Imhotep prowls the streets of Cairo in search of his lover's soul until a ray from the statue of a goddess burn's his life-giving scroll and he crumbles into a heap of bones.

THE BLOB!

The movie *The Blob* was about a giant, red, jelly-like creature that landed from outer space, and terrorized everyone with its nasty habit of rolling around engulfing and eating anything that got in its path. The Blob was made of silicone and the special effects team on the movie colored the Blob redder and redder the more people it consumed!

POD PEOPLE

Pod people were wandering extraterrestrial bodysnatchers whose planet had run out of resources. So they floated off as spores or seeds to colonize other planets, including Earth. Their plant pods took over humans at night, replacing them with identical but emotionless duplicates – while the original humans crumbled to dust. This spooky sci-fi scenario from *The Bodysnatchers*, a 1955 book by Jack Finney, has been made into a movie an astonishing 7 times.

KILLER VEGETATION

The Triffids are plants that want to take over the world. They move about on three "legs" so they can feed on the rotting bodies of dead humans, which they kill with a venomous sting. This chilling alien vegetation was dreamed up by writer John Wyndham in *The Day of the Triffids* and has been made into many movies and TV series – it's even spawned a comic strip.

HUNGRY KILLER JELLY!!

ZOMBIE ATTACK!

In *Things To Come* (1936), a highly contagious viral plague – "the wandering sickness" – drives the infected to wander about like mindless zombies possessed by spirits, infecting others upon contact. Zombie movies have been around since the 1960s, when *Night Of The Living Dead* became one of the most famous sci-fi movies of all time. The zombies usually look the same – relentless, slow-moving beings with rotting flesh and open wounds, dripping blood as if they've just been feasting on human bodies.

THE MARTIANS HAVE LANDED!

In 1898, author H. G. Wells wrote *The War Of The Worlds*, the first sci-fi book in which Earth was invaded by aliens. His Martians – plump, many-legged creatures – landed in meteor-like cylinders and immediately set up enormous three-legged fighting machines that decimated the humans around. Spooky red weed – a Martian vegetation – spread out over the land, and it seemed that earthlings were doomed. In 1938, U.S. actor Orson Welles broadcast *The War of the Worlds* on the radio and caused mass hysteria and panic, as thousands of people listening thought Earth really had been invaded by aliens.

Nice Alien

Not all aliens are bad. Vulcans from the *Star Trek* series are logical, kind and reasonable, and like to "mind-meld" or share their thoughts, emotions, and experiences with humans. You can spot them by their pointed ears and upswept eyebrows. They have copper in their blood, which means their skin often has a greenish tinge.

CROCODILE SCARS

Tribes living along the Sepik River in Papua New Guinea, in the south-western Pacific Ocean, initiate boys into manhood by carving the detailed design of a crocodile into the skin on their bodies. The design usually covers the whole of the back. They use a razor to carefully cut the design, which includes the scales of a crocodile's back.

SPECIAL ORDEALS

Initiation rites are often frightening or gruesome rituals that mark significant events, such as officially becoming an adult, or joining a group or society, such as a religious sect, a fraternity, a secret society, or a military unit. Usually they involve some sort of awful ordeal to test whether the person is worthy of being allowed to join the group. For example, young men in Brazil's Amazonian rainforest have to squirt poison in their own eyes before they are allowed to hunt.

WOW! IN BALI, YOUNG MEN FILE THEIR TOP FRONT TEETH TO SHARP POINTS WHEN THEY BECOME ADULTS.

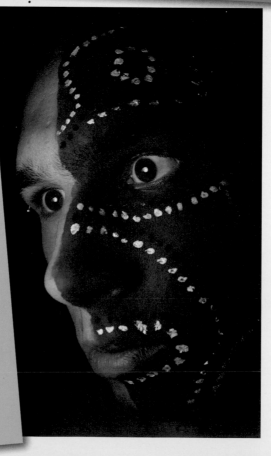

WILD WALKABOUT

In traditional Australian Aboriginal culture, teenage boys are sent on "walkabout" to live completely by themselves in the dangerous Australian Outback, which is extremely hot and full of killer insects and animals. They are sent into the wilderness for up to 6 months and walk the "Songlines," the ancient ceremonial pathways of their ancestors. The boys learn how to survive, hunting and killing animals, while coming to terms with their extreme loneliness. When the boys return, they are considered to have become men.

STINGING ANT GLOVES

The Sateré-Mawé people of the Amazonian rainforests make their young men wear gloves filled with venomous stinging ants. The bullet ants are so called because their sting is so powerful it feels like getting a bullet. The ants are sewn into wicker gloves, which the young men must wear while dancing for around 10 minutes. It sounds bad enough to do this once, but the boys must go through the ceremony 20 times.

CROSSING THE EQUATOR

It is traditional for sailors who cross the Equator for the first time to have to "kiss the Royal Belly." A senior member of crew who has a big stomach smears his belly with an unpleasant gooey mixture of mustard, raw eggs, shaving foam, cooking oil, and oysters. The first-timer has to kneel down in front of the belly and their face is smeared in the gunk.

COLLEGE FRATS

American colleges have fraternities and sororities, some called "Greek letter organizations," which have initiation ceremonies when a new member wants to join. This can involve extreme "hazing" or ritual bullying, including physical abuse, alcohol abuse, and dares. In 2002, 2 people died in an Alpha Kappa Alpha sorority or sisterhood ritual. Hazing is outlawed in 44 states, but it still goes on.

FREEMASON MYSTERIES

The secrecy surrounding the Freemasons has led people to claim that Jack the Ripper, one of the most notorious serial killers in history, was never discovered because he was protected by his fellow Freemasons in the police and judiciary. Freemasonry is an extremely old order, created in Europe about 500 years ago, which is also popular in the United States. Its members, who are all male, vow to help each other, and have to undergo secret initiation rites involving blindfolds and rolled-up trouser legs.

FIRST NATION SWEAT

Many Native American nations and tribes have held initiation ceremonies to mark the move into manhood. The elders of the tribe would teach a boy about the responsibilities of being a man. The boy would have his first session in a sweat lodge, a ceremonial sauna which reached incredible temperatures, usually in the dark. Some Native American boys would be sent out into the wilderness to fend for themselves for a period. After the initiation, the boy would be given a new name.

HALF A WRIGGLER

There are 34,000 different types of worms. The most common is the earthworm. It is not true that when an earthworm is cut in half it becomes two worms. One half (containing its "saddle" of vital organs) will survive, but the other half will die after wriggling about for a while. The living half sometimes grows new segments.

TOXIC WASTE WORM

The giant tube worm is capable of living in toxic waste, without any daylight, on the very bottom of the Pacific Ocean. It lives so far down in the murky depths that it does not have any predators. The giant tube worm can survive hardships which would kill most other species. It lives in sulfurous hot springs that can reach temperatures of 400°C (752°F).

DISGUSTING DISGUISE

Dung is important to many caterpillars. Some moth caterpillars feed from dung, while swallowtail caterpillars have the ability to disguise themselves very realistically as bird droppings to stop anything wanting to eat them. Other caterpillars can throw their own dung 1.5m (5ft) from their bottoms.

MONSTER WORMS

Some worms are incredibly long. The African giant earthworm can grow up to 6.7m (22ft), while the bootlace worm, which lives in the sea near the coasts of Britain, can be a shocking 60m (197ft) long. It is one of the longest creatures in the world. When touched, the bootlace worm produces a slimy, thick mucus and a pungent smell.

YUK! AN EARTHWORM EXCRETES THE EQUIVALENT OF ITS BODY WEIGHT EVERY SINGLE DAY.

CAUGHT BY SLIME

Glowworms, which live in caves in Australia and New Zealand, use slime to catch their prey. A glowworm spins a nest of silk on the ceiling of a dark cave and hangs down dozens of threads about 35cm (14in) long. Each thread is covered with slimy mucous, which is sometimes poisonous. The glowworm glows to attract its prey, including moths and snails, which get trapped in the sticky threads. The glowworm then pulls the prey up to the ceiling and eats it. If there is a lack of prey, it will turn to cannibalism.

GHOST SLUG

Garden slugs are descended from snails. They are gray, black, or orange and since they no longer have the protection of shells, they have to produce large amounts of mucus to stop them from drying out. This mucus leaves a slime trail and also helps them climb vertical walls without slipping down. Most slugs eat rotting vegetation but the ghost slug, which reaches a length of about 6.5cm (2.5in), has very sharp teeth and likes eating earthworms instead. It got its name because it is white and only comes out at night.

WORMERIES

Some people have wormeries in their back gardens. A wormery is a large plastic bin which has thousands of small red and tiger worms writhing around inside – when you lift the lid you can see them all wriggling madly. Every day, the worms gobble up loads of smelly, rotting kitchen waste – they love food that is starting to decay. Quite quickly it comes out their other ends as thick, black worm poo, which is used as compost.

FLESH-EATING MAGGOTS

Maggots are the larvae of flies. They are wriggly and smelly, and sometimes hundreds can be found in rotten food or dead animals. Humans have put them to good use, though. In Europe, many anglers use live maggots as bait on their end of their hooks, hoping that a fish will be tempted to take a bite. In medicine, including in America today, live maggots are sometimes used to help clean wounds. The maggots eat the dead tissue around the wound, but leave the live tissue.

BUCKING BRONCOS

Rodeo riders have to stay on a bucking animal for only 8 seconds in a bull-riding contest – but lots of them don't manage that long! Some bulls are so aggressive and high-spirited they cause gruesome damage to humans. In 1995, rodeo rider Tuff Hedeman was riding a feisty bull called Bodacious. The bull jerked Hedeman down on to his head, breaking all the major bones in his face. But after reconstructive surgery, Hedeman was soon back on the bucking broncos.

SKYDIVING HORROR

In 1977, when skydiver Mark Mongillo jumped out of a plane over Florida at 1,100m (3,600ft), his parachute somehow wrapped itself around his legs like a blanket. When his reserve chute also failed to open, he plummeted to earth like a stone. Amazingly, he landed in a ditch in an orange grove to find himself still alive, though with a broken leg, fractured shoulder, and nasty internal bruising. After a few weeks in a Florida hospital, he was walking again.

FIRST BLOOD WAGON

When people get injured skiing, they're carried down the slope in a gruesomely named "blood wagon" – a piece of cloth stretched over a metal sledge. The name dates from the 1520s, when wounded soldiers were carried from the snow-covered battlefields in the horrifically bloody ongoing wars between Sweden and Denmark.

NIAGARA DAREDEVIL

Briton Matthew Webb was the first person to swim the English Channel in 1875. He was slathered in porpoise fat to keep himself warm during the choppy 22-hour crossing, during which he was stung by jellyfish and drank brandy to keep the pain away. After his Channel crossing, he started doing exhibition swims for money. In 1893, he tried to earn $19,250 (£12,000) by swimming across the whirlpools at the bottom of the Niagara Falls. While his supporters watched, he was sucked under by the swirling torrents. His bashed and battered body was found downstream 4 days later.

HiGH WHeeL ACTiON

US BMX legend Mat Hoffman is a professional vert rider, which means he does stunts on very steep ramps. He's had major surgery 16 times. Once he was in a coma for several hours and another time he "flatlined," or was presumed dead, when the heart monitor he was attached to stopped beeping. But the most gruesome injury he received was when he jumped 7m (23ft) in the air from the top of a 6.4m (21ft) high ramp. On landing, he ruptured his spleen and there was so much internal bleeding he was given just 20 minutes to live. He survived.

NiGHTMARe PUCK

Canadian ice hockey player Clint Malarchuk almost died when he got his throat slit by another player's blade. He was going lowdown for the puck when the player's blade sliced through the major carotid artery in his neck. He was bleeding profusely on the ice but luckily someone pinched the artery tight to staunch the blood flow and held it until doctors could reach him. It took more than 300 stitches to seal the wound, but Malarchuk was back playing a short while afterward.

SPeAReD!

French long jumper Salim Sdiri was impaled by a rogue javelin in 2007 at an athletics championship in Rome. He was minding his own business near the long jump area when Finnish javelin contestant Tero Pitkämäki speared him with a badly thrown javelin. The 10cm (4in) deep wound touched Sdiri's kidney and made a hole in his liver.

UGH!
3 CYCLISTS HAVE DIED WHILE COMPETING IN THE TOUR DE FRANCE.

PEG LEG

After a skirmish with the English, the pirate François le Clerc had his leg sawn off without any anesthetic, but he carried on murdering, stealing, and fighting. The 16th-century pirate from Normandy in France was known as Peg Leg because he had a wooden leg strapped to his stump. He was very brave and reckless: he was always the first to board an enemy ship, brandishing his cutlass. His specialty was capturing Spanish treasure ships in the Caribbean.

PIRATE RULES

Pirates are usually regarded as being lawless people who could do whatever they wanted, but they had to follow the captain's strict rules onboard the ship. The rules varied, but often a pirate caught trying to desert would be left stranded on a remote island and anyone who stole from the crew would have their nose and ears cut off.

THE RICHEST PIRATE

Sir Henry Morgan was the most successful pirate. He often worked with the British authorities while amassing a huge fortune. Born in Wales in 1635, most of his plundering was in the Caribbean, where he was even made governor of Jamaica. His most famous exploit was when he organized 36 pirate ships to launch an attack on Panama City. He ransacked and torched the city, tortured the inhabitants, and stole as many "pieces of eight" (Spanish silver coins) as he could get his hands on.

WALK THE PLANK

Stede Bonnet was a wealthy landowner in Barbados who turned to piracy and became known as the "the gentleman pirate." He and his crew originally worked for Blackbeard. He is sometimes credited with being the first pirate to make his prisoners "walk the plank." Most pirates just threw their prisoners overboard to drown in the sea.

TOOTHLESS ANNIE

Some women also became famous pirates. Anne Bonny, born in Ireland in the 1690s, was known as Toothless Annie. She sailed, dressed as a man, with the pirate Calico Jack Rackham (who invented the Jolly Roger skull-and-crossbones flag). When the crew found out she was a woman, she killed the ones who objected to her being allowed on the ship. She was a fierce fighter. When Calico Jack's ship was captured in 1720, she and another woman, Mary Read, were the last pirates to carry on fighting while the rest hid below deck. Jack was hanged, but Annie was pardoned.

SMELLY LODGINGS

Being a pirate was not a glamorous job. Most of them lived on small ships called schooners and conditions were very cramped and smelly. Food usually consisted of pickled meat and dry biscuits for months and months as the pirates waited for the opportunity to raid the treasures of merchant ships.

DOUBLE HANGING

Scotsman William Kidd was the most famous pirate during his own lifetime. He is thought to have buried huge amounts of treasure on Gardiners Island, New York, and other locations. The treasure has never been found. He was hanged in London in 1701, but the rope broke, so he was hanged again. His body was left dangling over the River Thames to deter other pirates.

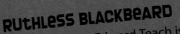

RUTHLESS BLACKBEARD

The Englishman Edward Teach is better known as Blackbeard and became notorious as the most bloodthirsty pirate to sail the seas. He is said to have tied slow-burning fuses to his braided black beard, giving him a frightening appearance. In 1718, he was shot 5 times and decapitated by Captain Robert Maynard and his men. Maynard hung Blackbeard's head from his ship.

COSMIC DEBRIS

There is a ring of man-made junk orbiting the Earth which is causing a problem. About a million bits of debris are estimated to be traveling round the Earth at speeds of up to 40,000kph (25,000mph). There is so much debris, including out-of-service satellites, pieces of rockets, and even astronauts' gloves, that it is starting to bang into spacecraft and may cause a major accident.

SPACE EXPOSURE

In order to survive in space, humans need to be in a specially pressurized vehicle or space suit. Humans cannot cope with the lack of normal air pressure in outer space and are likely to die within a minute of "space exposure." Many animals have died in tests carried out to discover the effects of space exposure.

SPACE TOILET

Going to the toilet on a spacecraft is a complicated, potentially messy problem because solids float in the absence of gravity. On a space shuttle, the solid waste is directed into a cylindrical container using air flow and rotating fans, and then dried to decrease its weight. However, the air has to be re-used in the cabin, so the astronauts have to breathe in the same air which is used to propel their waste. Luckily, the air is filtered first to remove the stinky odor and dirty bacteria.

BIG HAND

U.S. Air Force pilot Joseph Kittinger's hand blew up to twice its normal size when he parachuted from over 31,000m (100,000ft) in an astronaut's pressure suit. His right-hand glove failed to pressurize properly due to a faulty seal. The hand returned to its normal size after 3 hours of treatment back on Earth.

LUCKY 13

The crew of the Apollo 13 survived the most famous near miss in space history. In 1970, while on its way to the moon, a liquid oxygen tank ruptured and deprived the main craft of electrical power and its oxygen tanks. The crew was forced to use the craft's lunar module section in order to survive. Nobody knew if the crew would get back to Earth safely, but they succeeded.

SHUTTLE DISASTERS

The first time the U.S. suffered multiple in-flight fatalities on a space mission was in 1986. The space shuttle Challenger was destroyed due to structural failure caused by a faulty seal just 73 seconds after lift-off from the Kennedy Space Center in Florida. All 7 crew members died. The space shuttle Columbia, which had safely completed 27 missions, was destroyed on re-entry to the Earth's atmosphere in 2003, also killing its entire crew.

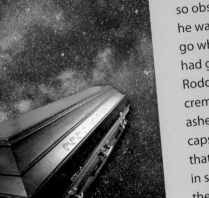

BURIED IN SPACE

The creator of *Star Trek* was so obsessed with space that he wanted his ashes to boldly go where no human remains had gone before. After Gene Roddenberry died he was cremated, and some of his ashes were sent up in a space capsule in 1997. It was hoped that his ashes would float in space for eternity, but the capsule lost height and disintegrated 7 years later. His family and friends are not giving up, though. They hope to send more of his ashes into deep space in the near future.

SPACE DEATHS

Going into space is fraught with danger, but only 3 people have died in outer space – when the cabin of the Russian Soyuz 11 spacecraft depressurized during its return to Earth in 1971. All the other space travel accidents have happened in the high atmosphere of the Earth or on the ground. In total, 22 astronauts have died, but there have been at least 170 ground crew and civilian deaths due to problems during launches.

MURAD THE HYPOCRITE

Many of the rulers of the Ottoman Empire, centered on modern-day Turkey, were wise and tolerant, but the 17th-century sultan Murad IV was brutal. He banned tobacco, alcohol, and even coffee in Istanbul. He used to dress up in normal clothes to walk the streets at night. If he saw anyone smoking or drinking, he would personally kill them with his mace. He died at the age of 27... as a result of drinking too much alcohol.

VLAD THE IMPALER

Vlad the Impaler, who ruled part of Central Europe in the 15th century, was the inspiration for Dracula the vampire. He got his nickname from having at least 20,000 of his 80,000 victims impaled on stakes.

GHASTLY GENGHIS

The Mongol Empire is the second largest empire in history. In the 13th century, it covered Eastern Europe and spread across the whole of Asia to the Pacific Ocean. The Mongols' gruesome leader was Genghis Khan, a great but vicious warrior. He slaughtered 200,000 people when he overran the ancient cities of Samarkand and Bukhara. In total, he killed at least 5 million people in order to set up his empire.

SHOCKING SISTERS

The daughters of English King Henry VIII hated each other's religions. Catholic Queen Mary became known as "Bloody Mary" for burning 300 Protestants, including the Archbishop of Canterbury, at the stake. Her sister, Protestant Queen Elizabeth, thought that Catholics were plotting against her, so she made the religion virtually illegal.

QUEEN OF DEATH

Queen Ranavalona of Madagascar was also known as "Bloody Mary of Madagascar" and the "Mad Queen." She killed half the population of her small country, mainly through torture. As soon as she came to power in 1828 she annihilated her dead husband's family, legalized the slave trade, and started to persecute all foreigners and Christians. Her favorite torture was to boil people alive.

TERRIBLE TYRANT

It is said that the Russian leader Ivan the Terrible liked the design of his new church, St. Basil's Cathedral in Moscow, so much that he had the architect blinded so that he could never design anything so beautiful again. When he decided he did not like the wealthy people of Novgorod, he burned the city and murdered thousands of the richest people.

ATTILA THE HUN

The Roman Empire had some very horrid rulers but even the Romans were scared of Attila the Hun, who called him the "Scourge of God." He was emperor of the German Huns in the 5th century. He attacked vast areas of the late Roman Empire, burning towns, ransacking monasteries, slaughtering priests, and murdering women.

MAD CALIGULA

The Emperor Caligula was even crazier than the infamous Nero. He killed his enemies and his friends on a whim, tried to give his horse a powerful government position, and thought he was a god. At the gladiator games, he once had a section of the crowd slaughtered by wild animals because he was bored.

STINKY SNAKE

The hognose snake, which lives in the United States and Mexico, is a great actor. When it is threatened, it will roll on its back and play dead, with its tongue hanging out. The snake finishes the performance by emitting a really foul, rancid smell, and by releasing some excrement. Most of its predators give up in disgust and leave it alone.

STENCH OF ANGER

When a male elephant is in its "must" phase it is angry and it stinks. Must is a period of highly aggressive behavior, when the huge elephants go crazy and start attacking each other. About 300 humans a year are killed by elephants, nearly always by males in a must phase. The must is accompanied by a tremendous, intense stench. If you smell it, run.

OLD MUSK

The muskox gets its name from the rank odor of musk emitted by the males. The muskox has been causing a stink since the time of the mammoths, and has lived in North America for up to 200,000 years. It is vaguely related to the sheep, but looks like a small American bison. We may think that the males smell horrible, but the female muskox are attracted by the odor.

BODY ODORS

We might think that animals smell, but many animals can smell humans from miles away. Even though we wash ourselves clean, domestic animals such as dogs and cats can distinguish between us just by our smell. Rescue dogs are sometimes used to find lost people in the wilderness as they can follow a human scent for many miles.

PETREL STENCH

The giant petrel is nicknamed "The Stinker." The bird's ultimate defense mechanism is to vomit on its attacker. The vomit contains a pungent stomach oil which has an unbearable smell. The petrels like the oil, though. They feed it to their chicks as it is an energy-rich food source which helps the babies grow quickly.

SMELLY ATTRACTION

The giant African millipede secretes a sticking, smelly substance from its pores. This puts off most predators, but not the lemur. This primate, which lives exclusively on the island of Madagascar, likes the taste of the substance so much that it sometimes licks it off the millipede's body.

FOUL SPRAYERS

Don't be fooled by the hippopotamus's unusually large head, bug eyes, and short legs. It may look like a cuddly character but it is highly aggressive and dangerous. It also has a disgusting way of marking its territory. The males spin their tails while defecating so their poop is sprayed over a huge area.

ULTIMATE STINKER

The skunk is the most famous stinker in the world. It has stink glands in its bottom which it uses as a defensive weapon. Skunks spray a highly disgusting, sulfurous liquid at their attackers. The liquid, which can be smelt by humans from 1.6km (1 mile) away, can irritate the skin of the attacker and even temporarily blind them. As a result, the skunk's only major predator is the great horned owl, which has no sense of smell.

WOW! A GHOST IN WILDENSTEIN CASTLE ONLY APPEARS TO PEOPLE WHEN THEY'RE IN THE BATH!

GHOST SHIP

Visitors often report spooky happenings on board the old warship USS *Alabama*. A tall blond man has been seen striding around in naval uniform, metal hatches slam shut, footsteps echo, knocking noises rebound through the bulkhead, and a woman's earring was once tugged off by an invisible hand. During WWII, the boat's gun turret crew were mistakenly shot by their own side, and some people think that their unsettled spirits haunt the museum ship today.

BROWN LADY

This tormented apparition has been seen stalking the corridors of Raynham Hall in England for centuries. She usually wears a brown-brocade dress, her glowing, unearthly face has gruesome bloody sockets where her eyes should be, and she grins in a "diabolical manner." She's said to be Lady Dorothy Townsend, imprisoned by her vicious husband before dying in mysterious circumstances. Her image was caught on camera in 1936, making her the world's most famous ghost.

SCREAMING SOLDIER

Donnington Castle in England is said to be packed with ghouls. It's believed that an ethereal guard lives in the gatehouse, an eerie white dog races from the castle into the woods, and a ghostly green lady floats around the grounds. But the most horrifying apparition is said to appear in the woods, where an elderly Royalist soldier has a 17th-century lady trapped in a headlock, pulling her hair. When witnesses reported shouting at him to stop, he screamed at them, and when they ran toward him, both he and the woman vanished into thin air.

MONTREAL MURDER

Every seven years, people gather in Montreal, Canada to see if they can catch sight of Mary Gallagher's ghost. Her head was hacked off in 1879 by her jealous love rival Susan Kennedy, who chucked it into a bucket to show everyone. Mary's headless, tormented figure is said to be seen roaming the streets in a long black cape on each seven-year anniversary of her death.

SPECTRAL DANCER

Just two weeks after singer Michael Jackson's death, his ghost was said to be haunting the corridors of his home at Neverland. An eerie, Jacko-shaped shadow was inadvertently caught on camera by a TV crew. It is said to have danced some way along the corridor before disappearing.

HEADLESS HORRORS

The headless ghost of Edward II's favorite courtier, Piers Gaveston, is believed to haunt the battlements of ruined Scarborough Castle in England. He's said to try and trip up unsuspecting people so they fall to their deaths below.

HIDEOUS HIGHWAYMAN

As well as robbing them, highwayman Tom Black was devilishly cruel to his victims. So when he was captured and hanged, the terrified locals wanted him to be buried at a crossroads with a stake driven through his heart, to prevent him ever returning. Yet the myth is that he returned: sometimes the phantom of a swarthy, blood-covered highwayman with a broken neck has been seen wandering the streets of Bedford, England.

ROMAN RUINS

Phantom Roman soldiers have been seen marching through the cellars of the Treasurer's House in York. A plumber was installing a new central heating system there and heard a horn blowing. When he looked down, he saw a carthorse and several weary legionaries carrying swords and shields — though they were cut off below the knee. He thought the ghostly figures were marching along the old Roman road, buried some 45cm below the floor of the cellar.

DARK AGE SPONGES

No medieval surgeon would be without his sporific sponge, soaked in drugs like henbane and hemlock, which he clamped over the patients' mouths to knock them out before doing amputations.

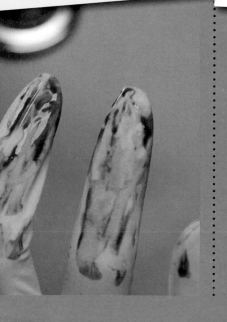

TAKING THE TEMPERATURE

Early thermometers were horrible to use. They were at least 30cm (12in) long and you had to keep one end in your mouth for 20 to 30 minutes before it would take a reading. Thermometers were also nasty germ-carriers, being used by sick person after sick person without being disinfected or washed.

BULLET EXTRACTOR

To take out bullets embedded deep in the body, surgeons used a special extendable bullet extractor. This slender metal instrument had a hollow rod containing a screw which could be lengthened by a handle. The end of the extractor was placed at the entry point, then extended into the body until it reached the bullet, when the surgeon pulled it out.

BRAIN SURGERY

By the 19th century, many types of hand-cranked brain drills and saws had been developed to cut swiftly through the skullbone and access the brain for surgery. Some had round blades, others worked like chainsaws. While drilling, surgeons stopped often to let the tools cool, as overheated metal could damage tender brain tissue.

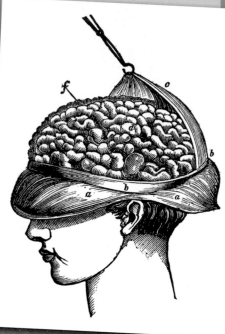

ANTS IN YOUR TUMMY

The weirdest surgical instrument is probably the giant ant. These little nippers with vice-like biting jaws were used to clamp the edges of intestinal wounds together, as even after death they won't let go! Doctors positioned the ants along the wound and, once they'd bitten it shut, would chop off their bodies leaving their heads still attached. The intestines would be pushed back into the stomach, which was sewn up, leaving the ants' heads to dissolve inside.

LeeCHiNG MACHiNe

For centuries, bloodletting – cutting veins and letting them bleed – was the first-line treatment offered to most sick people. Instead of doing it by hand, some doctors used an artificial "leeching" machine. This was a metal cylinder with several rotating blades at one end. The blades made cuts in the skin, then blood was quickly extracted by the vacuum created by the cylinder.

AMPUtatiON KNiFe

Being operated on in the 18th century was terrible. The surgeon's favorite tool was a long, horribly curved amputation knife which made a circular cut round the flesh and muscle of the limb to reach the bone, which he would then saw through. No surprises that around half of the people operated on died from blood loss or infection.

TONSiL GUiLLOtiNe

In Victorian times, people whose tonsils kept getting infected could have them removed with a double tonsil guillotine, which sliced out both tonsils at once. It had circular metal ends through which the tonsils were placed, then a small spring blade flashed across to cut through the skin behind.

WHAt A MOUtHFUL!

Barber surgeons extracted rotten teeth using a "tooth key." This was a doorkey-shaped metal rod with a claw at the end which was placed on the root of a tooth. The surgeon would fix the claw on the bad tooth, turn the key as if opening a door, and hopefully pull the whole tooth out.

RAT TEMPLE

In Deshnoke in India there's a Hindu temple swarming with 20,000 rats, which are treated as sacred. People come to make offerings to the rats, and when the rodents climb all over people it's considered a blessing. Even the water the rats drink is treated as holy. The temple is devoted to Karni Mata, a Hindu goddess. She is said to have turned her people temporarily into rats so they could escape the clutches of Yoma, the god of death.

GHOST TOWN

America has many abandoned, or "ghost," towns but one of the creepiest is Centralia in Pennsylvania. The streets are overgrown, the ground smolders and smokes, and there are warning signs about toxic emissions on every corner. Underneath the ground is a coal seam which was mistakenly set on fire 40 years ago by locals – and it's still burning today. Every single person had to leave town, for fear of turning into a human fireball!

YUK!
BAHRAIN HAS OVER 100,000 BURIAL MOUNDS PACKED WITH 6,000-YEAR-OLD BONES.

BONE CHAPEL

The small chapel of Sedlec in the Czech Republic is one of the world's most gruesome buildings. Inside, every inch is decorated with human bones. Garlands of skulls adorn the ceilings, a chandelier made from every bone in the human body hangs from the roof, and there is even a skeletal coat of arms on the wall. The bones of around 40,000 people buried in the graveyard were used to create this unusual interior in the 1870s.

SIBERIAN WASTE

One spooky place is Tunguska in remotest Siberia, Russia. It's a lonely, desolate spot with ancient blackened tree stumps and stunted vegetation. In 1908, a powerful explosion burned and flattened over 80 million trees and laid waste to 2,000 sq km (830 sq m). Some people thought an alien airship had landed, or that a meteorite had hit Earth, though there was no crater or impact hole. Today, scientists believe the gruesome burning and desolation seen on the ground was caused by the shock waves of an asteroid which exploded into watery fragments in the atmosphere.

PAINTED SKULLS

In a crypt in the small Austrian town of Halstatt, rows and rows of painted skulls make a very spooky sight. By the 12th century, the cemetery in this mountainous region was so full that people decided bodies could be buried there for only 15 years before being dug up. The bones were disposed of but the skulls were left in the sun to bleach, finding their final resting place in the crypt. From the late 18th century, families of the dead started painting the skulls with flowers, and adding their relative's name, date of birth, and death on them.

VAMPIRE'S LAIR

Poenari Castle, sitting high in the snow-covered mountains of Transylvania, has a grim and deadly past. It was the fortress home of Count Vlad Tepes, also known as Vlad the Impaler, and the inspiration for the mythical figure of Count Dracula. Poenari Castle is said to be one of the world's most gruesome places. Hundreds of slaves worked to death in the 1450s to rebuild it for the Count, and he tortured scores of people in its dungeons. His favorite method of murder was by impaling people on a stick through their bottoms – an end which the Count's wife also apparently met on this very site.

USE YOUR OWN!

Don't use other people's toothbrushes – they will be covered in bacteria, and sometimes with nasty cold, flu, and even measles viruses, too. These sorts of germs can survive for 48 hours or more on a dry toothbrush. And if you place two wet toothbrush heads together so they touch, the germs can move from one to another and carry infection across!

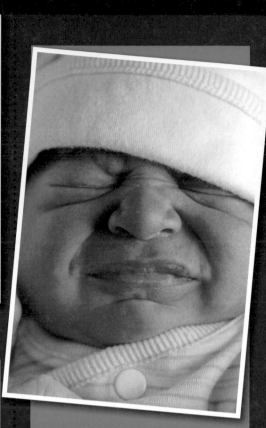

SWEATY FEET

Feet can be pretty pongy, too. That's because there are so many sweat glands on the soles – about 600 per square centimeter. Amazingly, the average male foot drips about 300ml (10fl oz) of sweat a day.

BORN SENSITIVE

Babies are born being able to sniff out nasty pongs. At just one day old, they make gruesome facial expressions of dislike when they're given decaying fish or rotten egg odors to smell.

THE WORST JOB IN THE WORLD?

How would you like to smell people's bad breath for a living? That's what a human odor judge does. They sniff out the chemical compounds that cause the whiffiness of bad breath. The worst offenders are hydrogen sulfide, which smells like rotten eggs, methyl mercaptan (cabbagey-poo), cadaverine (corpses), putrescine (rotting meat), and skatole (poo). Luckily for the judges, machines have now been designed to do this nasty job, too.

Excessive Sweating

Most people lose around 0.5l (17fl oz) of sweat a day, but sweat glands can produce 12l (405fl oz) a day if it's very hot. About 1% of people say they sweat excessively, and it can be very embarrassing for them. To ease the condition, doctors can inject a lethal poison called botulinum toxin (also known as Botox) into the armpit area. This stops or reduces sweating for about 6 months, when it has to be done again.

↖ SMELLY T-SHIRT

YUK! TONSILLOLITHS ARE SMALL, YELLOW, FOUL-SMELLING "STONES" THAT LIVE AROUND THE TONSILS AND CAUSE BAD BREATH.

Bacterial Stew

Most healthy people have up to 10 million bacteria rattling around in their mouths. But those with dental decay and other mouth infections can have 150 million or more in there! Some live in the dark spaces around the teeth and gums but most can be found on the tongue – especially at the back.

What Causes B.O.?

Sweat itself isn't smelly; it's the bacteria that feast on it that cause the whiff. Most body odor comes from the armpit and groin areas, especially after puberty. This sweat is rich in protein and, when bacteria break it down, it gives off a pungent pong. On other areas of the body there is more salt in the sweat, which bacteria don't break down in the same stinky way. That stale, dried B.O. smell usually happens when people don't wash their clothes after they've sweated in them, so the bacteria keeps ponging on.

Fish Odor Syndrome

Some people's sweat, breath, and urine gives off an incredibly strong fishy smell. This is called fish odor syndrome or trimethylaminuria (say it "try-meth-ill-amin-yuria"). It's an inherited syndrome in which the body is unable to break down certain ingredients in food, so they are eliminated as a fishy pong instead. There is no cure. To get rid of the odor, sufferers have to stop eating the foods their body can't process, such as egg yolk, lentils, some meats, milk, oranges, and soybeans.

FLYING DINOSAURS

The massive Quetzalcoatlus was probably the biggest flying animal that ever lived, swooping down from the sky and devouring smaller animals with its huge, vicious beak. It had an unusually long, stiff neck and an incredible wingspan of 11m (37ft) – about as long as a double decker bus!

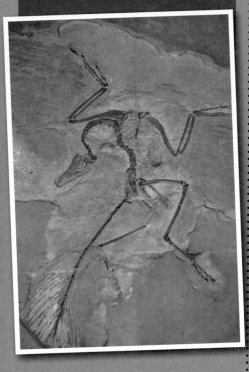

KILLING MACHINES

The raptors were the ultimate killers in the age of the dinosaurs. The Velociraptor was only about 2m (6ft) tall, but was very aggressive and hunted larger prey in packs. The dinosaur used its curved claws to pierce the throat to sever veins, arteries, and the windpipe. The Velociraptor's ancestor, the Utahraptor, was about 3 times its size but became extinct first.

LAND OF THE DINOSAURS

Dinosaurs roamed the Earth from about 220 million years ago until they became extinct about 65 million years ago. Dinosaurs came in all shapes and sizes, and many of them were aggressive killing machines, slicing or grinding their food with super sharp stacks of teeth.

HUGE CROCODILE

The Sarcosuchus, a type of monster crocodile, had 132 teeth as sharp as "railroad spikes," perfectly designed to grab and hold its prey. Twice as long as a crocodile, it was up to 10 times as heavy, and kept growing till the end of its life! About 12m (39ft) long and weighing 85kg (187lb), the Sarcosuchus lived in Africa about 110 million years ago.

ANCIENT KILLER SHARK

The Kronosaurus was a huge 10m (33ft) long dinosaur. Like a killer shark, it speedily hunted down its prey, including large fish and other marine reptiles, ripping them to shreds with long, sharp teeth. It is named after the most frightening Ancient Greek god, Kronos, who ate his own children.

THE TYRANT KING

The savage Tyrannosaurus Rex, or "tyrant lizard king," had a massive skull and a long, heavy tail. It could sniff out carcasses over vast distances, crushing their bones with its teeth. It measured up to 15m (50ft) and weighed 60,000kg (132,277lb) – by comparison the largest-ever elephant weighed 12,000kg (26,455lb). The almost intact remains of a T. Rex – nicknamed "Sue" – were found in South Dakota in 1990. Did "Sue" die of a bite to its head, as scientists suggest? We'll never know …

LARGEST VEGETARIANS

The biggest dinosaurs in the world – the Seismosaurus, Bruhathkayosaurus, and Argentinasaurus – ate tons and tons of vegetation every day, so it would be best to stand clear when they went to the toilet. They used their unbelievably long necks to poke deep into forests for their food. The Argentinasaurus was such a massive predator that it probably wolfed down other smaller or sick Argentinasaurus for lunch.

DINO CANNIBALS

The Majungatholus has a very bad reputation because its teeth marks have been found on the bones of other members of the same dinosaur species. Either it used to hunt down, attack, and eat its own relatives, or it used to feast on their remains once they were dead.

ULTIMATE DEFENSE

The Ankylosaurid was built like a war-tank! This "dinosaurian tank" was covered with plating made of thick bone, spikes, and lumps. Some even had armored eyelids. Its tail ended in a huge club with which it could strike a bone-crunching blow. Such incredible defenses, however, did little for its looks – it came to be known as the "fused lizard."

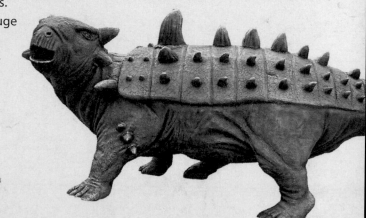

HERE COME THE NORMANS

It was because of the Vikings that the English lost the Battle of Hastings to the Normans in 1066. The English army was busy fighting the Vikings in the north of England when the Normans landed in the south. The English king, Harold, could not get enough troops to defeat the Normans. Harold died when he was shot in the eye with an arrow. The Normans took over England, and the country was changed forever.

YUK!!

FIERCE MEN OF SCANDINAVIA

The Vikings were fearsome people from Sweden, Denmark, and Norway who raided other countries from the 8th to the 11th centuries. They stole money and treasures, took prisoners, and murdered people as they tore through foreign lands.

MONK ATTACK

One of the first Viking raids on Britain was in AD 793, when they attacked the holy island of Lindisfarne on the north-east coast of England. The Vikings had no respect for the Christian monks. Some of the monks were made to become slaves while others were stabbed or drowned. The Vikings had their own non-Christian religion and their favorite god was Thor, the god of thunder.

DRINKING FROM SKULLS

The Vikings were obsessed by war. They were so fearsome in battle because they were not scared of dying. They thought that if they died in heroic battle they would go to Valhalla, a heaven where they would fight all day and drink from the skulls of their defeated enemies at night.

EATING SEAGULLS

The Vikings would eat any type of meat they could get their hands on, including horse, walrus, moose, whale, polar bear, and even seagull. They would often use the fur and skins to make clothes and blankets. They also liked to eat seaweed and drank mead and beer out of animal horns.

VIKING FUNERALS

The wives of the Vikings who plundered and then settled in Russia paid the ultimate price when their husbands died. They would be killed during the funeral so that they could accompany their husbands to Valhalla. Rich Viking warriors were so proud of their fast longboats that when they died, usually as a result of a ferocious battle, they would be buried inside their boats. Some of their slaves would also be murdered and buried with the warrior, along with their best weapons.

GIANT VIKING MYTHS

The Vikings believed in huge, frightening giants. They thought that the very first man and woman were created out of the sweat from under the armpit of a giant and that the clouds were the brains of a deceased giant. They also believed that thunder was the sound of the god Thor riding across the sky in his chariot.

MURDERER'S GUTS

Sometimes the Vikings received a taste of their own medicine. A ruthless Viking called Brodir wanted to kill the Irish king Brian Boru, who was a respected holy man. Against his own brother's wishes, Brodir slaughtered Boru before he could defend himself. As a punishment for the murder, Brodir had his stomach cut open and he was left to die slowly, with his guts spilling out.

DEATH OF EDMUND

In AD 869, King Edmund of England decided to try to convert the Vikings to Christianity rather than fight them. The Vikings did not like this idea. They captured Edmund, beat him, tied him to a tree, shot him with arrows, cut him up, and beheaded him.

FEED ME!

A monster man-eating plant plans to take over the world in the musical movie, *Little Shop Of Horrors*. The plant started off small but then Seymour, who discovered it in the florist's shop, found out it had rather a strange appetite. It liked human blood and flesh and kept saying "Feed me!" He called the carnivorous plant Audrey II, and kept feeding it his own blood until it grew enormous. Eventually, it could eat humans whole – and munched down the dentist and shop owner with no problems at all.

RED DEATH

In the spoof movie *Attack Of The Killer Tomatoes*, tomatoes rise up against humankind and start rampaging around the world. These vegetables of doom grow to giant proportions and kill people while they're putting out the garbage or swimming, poisoning them with toxic tomato juice or squashing them flat and leaving trails of red watery juice everywhere instead of blood.

FAMILY HORROR

Uncle Fester of *The Addam's Family* is a horror! Bald, stooping, with spooky sunken eyes and a mad smile, he likes to play gruesome tricks such as turning the shower setting to "scalding," pouring boiling oil on carol singers, and feeding his pot plants blood. He also has an uncanny ability to conduct electricity, and can light a bulb in his mouth with a loud crackling noise. Not much worries him, not even a crack on the head from a cannonball. In fact, for fun, he likes to put his skull in an enormous screw handle press and turn hard!

ACTORLY ENDS

An actor decided to get rid of all the critics who'd ever ridiculed his performances – by killing them in gruesome Shakespearean-inspired deaths. In the movie *Theater Of Blood*, one critic was stabbed like Julius Caesar, another was tricked into eating his beloved poodles in a pie (as in *Titus Andronicus*), and another was electrocuted by her hair curlers (burnt to death like Joan of Arc in *Henry VI Part I*). It's said that 27 liters (6 gallons) of fake blood were needed to stage the murders.

KING OF THE MONSTERS

Godzilla is a mutant dinosaur who rampages around killing humans who cross his path. Nuclear testing in the Pacific created this self-replicating monster, which has legs like a Tyrannosaurus Rex, a plated backbone like a Stegosaurus, and the thick scaly skin and tail of a crocodile. He's superstrong, fierce, and intelligent – and wants to take over the world. One of his most powerful weapons is his "atomic" breath – his dorsal fins start glowing and he shoots a blast of fiery energy which destroys everything it touches.

MUCK MONSTER

Swamp Thing was a gruesome man-turned-monster which lived in the muck and filth of the Louisiana swamps. Originally a scientist called Alec Holland, Swamp Thing mutated after being poisoned with strange chemicals and dumped in the swamps by the evil Dr. Anton Arcane. No longer human or animal, but a mass of vegetable matter with a very deep voice, he raced round trying to protect people in the U.S. TV series *Swamp Thing*.

MAN-FISH

One of the creepiest monsters is "Gill-man." He's half-man, half-fish, with enormous webbed hands and sharp claws which he uses to rip apart humans who get in his way. His strength is superhuman, he can live on land or in water, and his scaly skin is so tough and resilient that even fire can't hurt him. This prehistoric amphibian lives deep in the unexplored Amazonian rainforest, and starred in *Creature from the Black Lagoon*.

LUCKY GUINEA PIG

Medical student Stubbins Ffirth believed that the killer disease yellow fever was not contagious. So he concocted some revolting experiments to try out on himself. He rubbed "fresh black vomit" from a victim into cuts on his body. No problem. He smeared infected blood, spit, sweat, and urine all over himself, including in his eyes. He stayed well. He even ate victims' just-spewed sick. He didn't get yellow fever and concluded that it was not contagious. But in fact he was very wrong (and very lucky), for the disease is transmitted directly into the bloodstream.

DANGEROUS NEWTON

Brilliant mathematician Isaac Newton discovered the force of gravity when he saw an apple fall to the ground from a tree. But many of his other experiments were extremely dangerous – to himself at least. While trying to find out about the way we see color, he nearly blinded himself by poking sharp objects into his eyes, and he stared so hard at the sun's reflection in a mirror that his eyes were said to be scarred.

DOUBLE EXPLOSIVE

When Pierre Louis Dulong mixed some chemicals together he made an oil called nitrogen trichloride which exploded violently, losing him three fingers and an eye. Someone sent news of the experiment to English chemist Humphry Davy and, in the spirit of scientific inquiry, he repeated the experimental explosion – almost losing his eye!

YUK! ALCHEMISTS USED TO TASTE THEIR DISTILLATIONS, AND OFTEN POISONED THEMSELVES WITH TOXIC METALS.

EAR MITES AND MEN

Veterinarian Dr. Robert Lopez wanted to find out if pets' itchy ear mites can live on humans too. So he put some into his own ears. He experienced "a weird cacophony of sound and pain" as the mites moved and scratched, which made it impossible for him to sleep. The infestation cleared up in about a month, so he infected himself again, and again – each time the symptoms were milder, which made him think that both people and animals might become immune.

GAS ATTACKS

British biologist J. B. S. Haldane regularly gassed himself with methane, chlorine, nitrogen, carbon monoxide, and mustard gas – all to find out how the body responded to gases under pressure. He used to turn blue and pass out in the decompression chamber, and have seizures from the lack of oxygen. He often burst his eardrums but didn't seem to mind that either, saying that it was a "social accomplishment."

TRIPLE SICK

18th-century biologist Lazzaro Spallanzani had an enquiring mind and wanted to find out what happened to food once it was inside the body. So he conducted a gross experiment in which he ate some food, sicked it up, ate the vomit, sicked that up, ate the regurgitated vomit – you get the picture. He found out that it gets runnier and runnier each time.

WEIGH IN

In the 16th century, Santorio Santorio conducted a bizarre experiment on himself. He weighed everything that went into his body – food, drink, and so on – and everything that came out – wee, poo, and so on. For years, he lived on a weighing platform suspended from a large balance, rather like enormous weighing scales. By this method he discovered that humans perspire, losing body weight through sweating.

YEAR WITHOUT A SUMMER

When Mount Tambora in Indonesia erupted in 1815, what sounded like terrifying gunfire was heard 2,576km (1,600 miles) away in Sumatra! The whole mountain turned into a flowing mass of "liquid fire" and the eruption caused a shift in the climate of the northern hemisphere which led, in 1816, to the so-called "year without a summer." Snow fell that June in New York, and Europe experienced the worst famine of the 19th century.

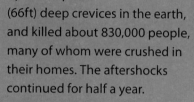

DISAPPEARING EARTH

The Shaanxi earthquake in China, 1556, was one of the most violent in history. It threw the ground up violently to form new hills, triggered landslides, opened up 20m (66ft) deep crevices in the earth, and killed about 830,000 people, many of whom were crushed in their homes. The aftershocks continued for half a year.

TOWN OF ASH

In AD79, the volcano Vesuvius erupted violently, burying the Roman city of Herculaneum in mud and covering the town of Pompeii with a 20m (66ft) layer of volcanic ash. The quake lasted for over 19 hours, blocking out the sun as people ran with pillows tied to their heads to protect their skulls from being fractured by flying rocks and roof slates. The ash preserved the town – and some of the bodies of its inhabitants – exactly as at the time of the eruption.

SWALLOWING SAND

Quicksand is absolutely terrifying. It is sand that appears to be solid enough to walk on, but when you step on it you start to sink and the ground begins to swallow you up, dragging you under. It can be virtually impossible to extract yourself from quicksand as there is nothing solid to push against. Even if the person stuck in the sand is not completely sucked under, they face drowning when the tide comes in, or death from long-term exposure to hot sun.

FARE! Kviksand
DANGER! Quicksand
ACHTUNG! Quicksand

An Infestation of Snakes

The Caribbean volcano Mount Pelée, dormant for centuries, erupted in 1902 killing 30,000 people. For 9 days prior to the catastrophe, the mountain heaved, rained ash over the city of Saint Pierre below, and spat boulders and trees into the rivers. Animals seemed to know disaster was on the way and tried desperately to make their escape down the mountainside. The streets of Saint Pierre were invaded by speckled ants, centipedes 30cm (1ft) long, and hundreds of nasty fer-de-lance snakes that slithered around biting people and animals.

Great American Flood

In 1889, Johnstown, Pennsylvania saw one of the worst floods in American history. Dams and viaducts gave way, boilers exploded, creeks turned into raging torrents that uprooted trees and homes, telegraph lines were submerged, rail tracks washed away. The waters rose to 3m (10ft) high, killing 2,200 people and leaving bare waste and rock where once had stood streets and homes. People not crushed by the debris were caught in barbed wire as a wire factory upstream was washed away. So great was the devastation, they needed dynamite to clear it.

Dutch Disaster

In 1287, more than 50,000 people died in the horrific St. Lucia's flood in the Netherlands. The country is almost completely flat, with surrounding water held back by a series of huge dikes that are sometimes breached in wild weather. A dike broke during a terrible storm and thousands of people drowned within hours. Only 10 houses were left standing on the island of Griend, which has now been abandoned.

SPONGE WARFARE

Dirty washing-up sponges are havens for bacteria. In 8 hours, just one single bacterium can multiply to 16 million given the right damp, warm conditions. Every time a surface is wiped with a dirty cloth, it spreads the bacteria around – and most families don't change their sponge cloths often enough. In one study, only 20% of people changed their cloths once a month or more.

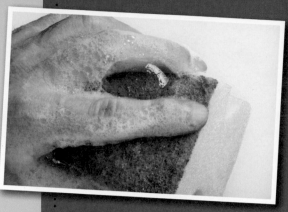

CELL PHONES

Every square inch of a cell phone is absolutely crawling with tens of thousands of microbes. Cell phones tend to be warm and are handled all the time, so provide a fantastic breeding ground for nasty germs that cause pimples, rashes, and even gruesome tummy bugs.

COOL GERMS

You'd think that refrigerators and freezers, by keeping things cool, would stop bacteria from growing inside them. But there are lots of micro-organisms called psychrophiles that thrive when it's cold in the refrigerator or freezer. These include some molds and listeria, which can cause nasty bouts of food poisoning with diarrhea, stomach cramps, and vomiting.

BED SHARERS

Have you ever wondered why bedlinen is usually white? In the olden days, people painted their bedframes white and used white linen so they could see bedbugs more easily – and then killed them by bashing them with bars of soap. These 3mm (⅛-in) long bugs infest bedding and mattresses and leave nasty, irritating bites on skin and a pongy, rotting smell in the room. Bedbugs can run up the legs of beds too, so people used to stand them in pans of liquid paraffin to drown them.

DUSTY STUFF

Dust is made up of dead skin, dust mites, dustmite poo, dead dust mites, bacterial microorganisms, mold spores, pet dander, and other debris – no wonder it gets right up people's noses. The dustiest place in a house is usually the bedroom. In a 6-year-old pillow, a tenth of the weight is likely to be made up of human skin scales, dust mites, dead and alive, and their droppings!

MUCK SPREADER

Cross-contamination is when harmful germs are spread to food from elsewhere. One of the most common ways it happens is by people not washing their hands after going to the toilet – then picking up something with their fingers and eating it. Parents with young babies often spread germs unknowingly when they change a nappy. They wash their hands – covered with germs from the poo – in the kitchen sink where vegetables are washed and food prepared. Cross-contamination can cause serious food stomach upsets, vomiting, and diarrhea, and sometimes even death.

DANDY PETS

Dander is the dead stuff shed by animals. It includes skin flakes, hair, dandruff, and feathers, but pets also produce other nasty substances like saliva and urine which can dry and float around in the air within a house or living area. Dander can linger for up to 6 months after the pet has disappeared, and around one in 10 people are allergic to it. It makes them sneeze or snuffle, or come out in rashes or red bumps.

PESKY MOTHS

It's not moths that make those holes in favorite jumpers – it's their babies. Moths lay the eggs that turn into the larvae which then munch their way through carpets, clothes, and curtains. They're most attracted to grimy, smelly items which have human oils and sweat on them.

GHOSTS A GO-GO!

With its 12 reported specters, the little village of Pluckley in Kent, England is one of the most haunted places in the world. There are said to be two ghosts in St. Nicholas church, bloodcurdling screams issuing from the brickworks, a spectral horse-drawn carriage complete with headless coachman trotting down the street, an eerie monk stalking the lanes, a dying highwayman hanging in a tree at Fright Corner – even the Black Horse Inn is said to have a mischievous poltergeist.

WHITE HOUSE SPECTERS

Many former U.S. presidents and their wives seem to haunt the White House. Abraham Lincoln is reportedly the most regular visitor, often standing looking out of windows with his hands behind his back. Andrew Jackson has been seen laughing in the Rose Bedroom; Thomas Jefferson and John Tyler stroll around the Yellow Oval Room; Dorothea Madison wanders through the Rose Garden; and William Henry Harrison is said to rummage in the attic.

GHOSTS OF GETTYSBURG

In the Battle of Gettysburg of 1863, around 46,000 soldiers died and 50,000 amputations were carried out. The first Gettysburg ghosts were reportedly seen a week after the battle. People believed they saw soldiers marching or fighting, a ghostly "General" walking down the street with his officers, and a Confederate cavalryman racing off on horseback. But the most spectacularly spooky sight was said to be an amputated soldier's arm dripping with blood on a windowsill.

HAUNTING HORROR

The most haunted house in the U.S.A. is said to be the Lalaurie Mansion in New Orleans, where for years people have reported strange noises, screams and groans, and terrifying phantoms such as a naked man in chains, a specter with a whip, shrouded figures, and the wraiths of slaves walking in the yard. It's said that the cruel owner, Madame Lalaurie, used to torture her slaves to death.

IRISH JIGS

Malahide Castle in Ireland is believed to have five vociferous ghosts, including a court jester dwarf and the gruesome Miles Corbett. Corbett was hung, drawn, and quartered. People say that although his ghost first appears as a figure in full armor, it then breaks into pieces before their eyes.

BURLINGTON BANSHEES

Blood-flowing statues, waitress ghouls, chimney sweep specters, and ethereal soldiers – the town of Burlington, Ontario, Canada is said to have them all. Many of the ghosts seem to live in restaurants, pubs, and bars – the Poacher pub alone is believed to have three! But the most gruesome spot is the war memorial, where the resident ghost has been heard talking to the statue of a WW1 soldier. The statue's mouth and eyes apparently open and close and his fingers are said to twitch on the rifle butt.

AUSTRALIA'S MOST HAUNTED

Hundreds of people with plague, cholera, and smallpox died in Sydney's Quarantine Station, and it's now said to be inhabited by many ghosts. But the most unusual is a little girl with long blonde plaits who's said to like nothing better than holding visitors' hands.

AMITYVILLE HORROR

When Ronald DeFeo shot his family dead in their home in Amityville on Long Island, U.S.A., he's said to have set off a horror story. The next owners were apparently plagued by poltergeists, demons, ghosts, swarms of flies, rotting smells, green slime bleeding from the walls, and a ghostly pig called Jodie with glowing red eyes. They left after 28 days of this supernatural hell.

DANISH BOOOOOO!

The notorious Danish castle of Dragsholm Slot is said to be home to over 100 ghosts, including that of Earl of Bothwell, Mary Queen of Scots' third husband. He was imprisoned and died here in appalling conditions, and his ghost has been seen riding round in a horse-drawn carriage. The most gruesome ghoul is the wailing White Lady who is said to stalk the corridors every night. When she fell in love with the wrong man, her father imprisoned her inside the walls of the castle, where she's believed to have starved to death.

Monster Bite

The gila monster is the only venomous lizard native to the United States. The large lizards often flip over while biting into a victim to help the venom flow from its saliva gland to its teeth. They do not usually manage to bite humans because they are so slow. If they do, the monster must be submerged under water to make them release their incredibly strong bite. Luckily, the venom is not fatal to humans.

Multi-Armed Defense

At only 18cm (7in) long, blue-ringed octopuses are small compared to most other octopus species, but they are one of the most venomous animals in the world. The octopus is usually quite docile, but it will give a human a vicious bite if stepped on or provoked. Its venom can kill a human and there is no known antidote.

Snail Harpoon

The cone snail is nature's quickest venomous killer. The snail launches a barbed harpoon out of its mouth to inject its prey with poison. The victim is paralyzed instantly. The snail retracts the harpoon and its attached prey back into its mouth.

Sea Killer

Sea snakes, which live in the coastal waters of the Indian and Pacific Oceans, are often highly venomous. Their venom is among the strongest of all animals, but luckily they do not usually use much of it when they bite a victim. A human who is bitten by a sea snake will get a headache and start vomiting, and their muscles will start to hurt. This can be followed by paralysis and kidney failure, and ultimately, after 6 to 12 hours, their heart stops.

KING OF VENOM

The fork-tongued king cobra is one of the most dangerous snakes in the world. It is the longest venomous snake, averaging 4m (13ft) long, and one drop of its venom is enough to kill 50 humans. The king cobra is very fast and aggressive, raising up its body and striking at speed as soon as it is irritated. Humans that are bitten usually die within 45 minutes.

DRAGON SLAYER

The komodo dragon, which has red saliva, has pouches of venom in its mouth which cause toxic shock and paralyze its prey. Scientists are not sure whether the venom is necessary ,as the komodo's huge size and flesh-ripping bite is usually enough to kill victims. In 2001, one man had his toe bitten off while petting a komodo dragon in a zoo.

KILLER FISH

The reef stonefish, so gnarled and ugly that it looks like a piece of rock, is the most venomous fish in the world. The venom is not stored in its mouth, but in 13 sharp spines sticking out from its back. The fish lives in shallow water, so it is sometimes accidentally stepped on by human bathers. This results in incredible pain, followed by death if the venom is not treated.

POISON FROG

The golden poison frog suits its name: it is golden in color and it is extremely poisonous. In fact, it is the most poisonous vertebrate in the world. It lives on the Pacific coast of Colombia, eating ants and termites. The poison on the frog's skin puts off predators. It can kill anything, even a huge elephant.

TORTURE CHAIR

One of the worst medieval tortures involved a chair which was completely covered in about 1,000 sharp spikes on the seat, back, armrests, and legs. Prisoners would be tied to the chair and the spikes would sink into the body. It could take a day to die in the chair of torture. The spikes were not long enough to pierce the vital organs, so the victim would slowly bleed to death. But most people confessed before they were made to sit down.

NOT A TORTURE CHAIR

THE ERA OF TORTURE

Medieval Europe was probably the most gruesome era in history. The rulers would happily have a victim tortured in order to make him confess to a crime. They carefully worked out how to do this as painfully as possible. They invented weird, cruel contraptions which would make people confess even if they had not done anything wrong.

THUMBSCREWS

Thumbscrews were not meant to kill a victim but would cause unbearable pain. The thumbs were put inside a metal vice, and a screw was tightened so that the thumbs became crushed. They were a favorite way to make someone confess in medieval Europe, but they were still being used on slaves in 18th-century America.

CATHERINE WHEEL

The prisoner would be tied to a large cart wheel known as the Catherine wheel or breaking wheel. The wheel was turned while the executioner aimed heavy blows with a metal hammer, breaking the victim's bones. If the executioner was merciful, he would kill the prisoner by smashing his chest. Otherwise, it could take days to die.

ALE DEPRIVATION

One old English torture was to deprive a convicted person of ale. This may not sound such a terrible punishment to us today, but in times past ale was the only drink available to many people, especially poor ones. Even children were given beer allocations – 1 liter (2 gallons) a week in one children's hostel in 1632. There was no running water in houses, and water supplies in urban areas could be contaminated with deadly diseases such as cholera. Not being able to drink ale was a torture of a gruesome – and perhaps even deadly – kind.

IRON MAIDEN

This was a hinged box, rather like a coffin, but with spikes on the inside of the door. The victim had to get inside the box and then the door would be forced shut so that the spikes would pierce the victim's flesh. The box often had a hinged opening so that the torturer could interrogate the prisoner as the torture progressed.

STRETCHED ON THE RACK

The rack was the most feared instrument of torture in medieval times. It was a frame on which the prisoner was made to lie down. The prisoner's feet were tied to the bottom of the rack, while the hands were chained to a roller at the top. The torturer would then turn a handle which made the roller move, stretching the limbs.

BURNT ALIVE

The Brazen Bull was invented by the Ancient Greeks but was still used in the Middle Ages, especially in Central Europe. The prisoner was made to get inside a hollow brass container shaped like a bull. A very hot fire was lit under the bull, which was heated up until it was almost white hot, burning the prisoner trapped inside. Its inventor, Perilaus, was the first person to feel its effects because his ruler, Phalaris, made him get inside.

GRUB-EATERS

The Kombai people of Indonesia know how to treat their special guests. They feed them huge, juicy grubs. The sago grub, which is the larva of the capricorn beetle, is the tribe's favorite food. A sago palm is cut down, wrapped in leaves, and left to rot for several weeks. The sago grubs feed on the palm, becoming big and juicy, at which point they are ready to become a wriggly meal.

SQUID ENTRAILS

The Japanese eat slippery, slimy squid entrails. Called shiokara, the squid is served in a salty, pink, muddy sauce, which is made out of the squid's digestive system, including whatever it last ate for dinner. The dish has a very powerful fishy taste and it is very chewy, so it is hard to swallow quickly even if you start to gag or your stomach starts to flip.

CAT-POOP COFFEE

Incredibly, the most expensive coffee in the world is made with the feces of a cat-like mammal. Kopi luwak, otherwise known as civet coffee, is a sought-after drink in the Philippines and Indonesia. Animals called Asian palm civets are fed coffee berries, but the beans inside the berries pass through their systems and end up coming out in their poo. The beans are then washed, roasted, and brewed for what must be the most gruesome cup of coffee in the world.

BIRD SPIT SOUP

In China, people eat revolting bird nests that are entirely made out of saliva. Certain types of swifts that live in caves build their nests by interweaving strands of their own spit. When the spit nests are dissolved in water, they create a slimy, sweet soup. The soup, which is very expensive, is thought to be extremely healthy, benefiting the immune system and even helping to prevent asthma. Some Americans import the nests for thousands of dollars per kilogram.

UGH!
A HIGH-CLASS CHINESE DISH INCLUDES A FISH WHICH IS COOKED AND EATEN WHILE STILL ALIVE.

SQUIRREL BRAINS

The sloppy brains of a squirrel have become a favorite delicacy in Kentucky. The squirrels are hunted rather than reared just for their brain-food. However, eating them can be extremely hazardous. Doctors have warned the squirrel-brain eaters that they could catch Creutzfeldt-Jakob disease, an incurable and fatal illness.

ROTTEN HORSE MILK

In parts of central Asia, they like to get drunk on foul-smelling, rotten horse milk. Mares are milked and then the milk is left to rot, becoming infested with bacteria. This fermentation gives the rotten milk an alcohol content. Some people prefer it to beer or wine.

CATERPILLAR FUNGUS

Caterpillar fungus is used as a gruesome ingredient in Chinese soup. The fungus infects the caterpillar and mummifies its body. It then grows a mushroom out of the caterpillar's head. Both the caterpillar and fungus are eaten as part of a cure in Chinese medicine, but the rotten wrigglers are also sometimes dropped in soups.

GAS ACCELERATORS!

Cabbages, mushrooms, beans, cauliflowers, broccoli, asparagus, and Brussels sprouts tend to make you fart more. They contain sugars that are hard to digest, so the bacteria in the gut have a party time and make loads of gas. Vegetarians who eat more of these foods tend to produce more gas than meat-eaters – though it's not necessarily all that smelly.

LETHAL PORTION!

SMELLY BURPS

Most burps are odorless, but occasionally out pops one that smells of rotten eggs, which is pretty nasty. It's usually because you've eaten a big meaty meal with lots of protein which your tummy is taking a long time to process – and belching lets some of the gas out.

FAMOUS "FARTiSTE"

Joseph Pujol was a hugely popular entertainer known as "Le Pétomane" (that's "fart maniac" in French) in 19th-century France. He had an incredible skill – he could expel air loudly through his bottom at will. He played tunes on the ocarina, blew out candles, imitated farmyard animals, and orchestrated thunderstorms and earthquakes. His talented rear end made him one of the best-paid entertainers of his time.

Reverse FARTING?

Some people think burps are the same as farts, just from the other end. But in fact they're quite different. Burping is caused by taking in too much air into the stomach while you eat – and quite often it pops up through the gullet and mouth as a big burp! If you have lots of fizzy drinks, or eat very fast, you'll find you belch more.

HOLDING THEM IN

Roman Emperor Claudius (10 BC to AD 54) was said to have been so worried about people politely holding in their farts and being poisoned by them that he passed a law legalizing farting at feasts. He was wrong: holding in farts won't make you ill. But strangely, it can make them less stinky. That's because some of the smellier gases are absorbed into the bloodstream through the gut walls, leaving more nitrogen – which doesn't smell as bad as many of the other gases –in the fart.

WHAT'S THAT PONG?

The smell of a person's farts depends on the mix of bacteria they have in their gut. And that depends on what was floating around when they picked it up as newborn babies. Throughout your life, your intestinal flora doesn't change that much – so if you tend to fart a lot of methane as a child, you're likely to do so as an adult, too.

YUK! MOST PEOPLE PASS AROUND 600ML OF GAS A DAY IN 14 FARTS!

SMELLY INVADERS

When you smell a fart, it means the poop gases are inside your nose. Your smell receptors are in the upper part of each nasal chamber – so to smell something means that it has invaded your nose space!

SILENT BUT DEADLY

The smelliest farts often come after you've eaten foods high in sulfur, such as eggs, seafood, beef, liver, chicken, peanuts, cheese, nuts, and seeds. Five main gases come out of your bottom – nitrogen, carbon dioxide, methane, hydrogen, and oxygen. The stinkiest farts are usually those with a high level of hydrogen sulfide in them – rotten-egg farts – from all the sulfur you've eaten.

HOME DELIVERY SERVICE

The burrowing owl, which lives in North and South America, loves dung. It lines its underground nest with all types of debris, but it is particularly fond of cow dung. The smell of the dung attracts the owls' favorite food, the dung beetle, right into the nest, where it becomes a quick snack.

THRUSH BOMBS

The fieldfare is only a relatively small bird, but it has a spectacular way of defending itself which deters even the most aggressive attacker. Fieldfares, which are a species of thrush about 24cm (10in) long, nest fairly close together. When a predator bird such as a crow enters the nesting area, all the fieldfares gang together to mob it, bombing the attacker with bird-droppings. The predator can become so covered with droppings that it cannot fly properly.

BIRDS OF PREY

Eagles are the ultimate birds of prey because they are large, powerfully built, fast, have great vision, and are very efficient killers. They are "raptors," which means they take their prey by force. They swoop down on their victims from the sky, grab them with their strong, sharp talons, and rip them apart with their hooked beaks. Many species of eagle lay two eggs. The larger chick usually kills the smaller one.

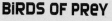

ROTTEN EATER

The vulture is the world's most gruesome bird. These large scavengers feed from the carcasses of dead or dying animals, no matter how rotten the meat has become. Vultures have extremely corrosive stomach acid which enables them to consume putrid, disease-infested flesh without any ill effects. They are often bald-headed so that messy bits of carcass do not become stuck around their faces.

FUNNY KICKER

The ostrich may be one of the most peculiar-looking birds on the planet, but it can also be one of the meanest. Native to Africa, ostriches have big bodies, long necks, and little heads, and its brain is smaller than one of its eyes. They can grow up to 2.8m (9ft) tall and an adult male can weigh a huge 155kg (340lb). They cannot fly but they are the quickest bird on land, reaching 70kph (45mph), and can keep running at this speed for half an hour. If they are cornered, they will attack. Their kicks are so strong they can cause serious injury or death, even to large animals like lions.

SEAGULL ATTACK

Seagulls sometimes act as if they are inspired by Alfred Hitchcock's famous horror film, *The Birds* (1963), in which birds violently attack humans. Flocks of seagulls can become fierce and brazen in their attempts to take food away from people, especially in established tourist areas. They often steal ice-creams from children's hands, and several people have been hospitalized by frenzied seagull attacks. Gulls will also attack fiercely if their young are threatened.

POOP ISLAND

The little island of Nauru in the South Pacific is absolutely smothered in bird excrement – guano. We may find that disgusting, especially for the 14,000 people who live there, but the poo is precious. Bird droppings contain natural phosphates that make it sought after for use in fertilizers. In fact, Nauru made its fortune from being poop island.

PECK YOUR EYES OUT

The crow is a vicious bird. Carrion crows have been known to kill newborn lambs and to feast on human corpses. In a recent incident in Bahrain, a 30-year-old man was attacked by a group of about 30 crows, and one jabbed its beak into his eye, leaving him severely injured. A group of crows is actually called a "murder."

SLINGS AND CATAPULTS

For thousands of years, siege warfare was one of the best military tactics to defeat an enemy. An army would surround a city and bombard it with weaponry, or cut off all food supplies so eventually the starving city would be forced to surrender. By the 20th century, siege warfare had virtually died out.

OTTOMAN FURY

The Turkish Ottomans captured Constantinople, the capital of the 1,000-year-old Byzantine Empire, after a horrific siege lasting nearly 2 months in 1453. The city tried to make peace with the Turks, sending ambassadors with gifts, but they were executed. Around 100,000 soldiers surrounded the city, which had a force of just 7,000 men. The defenders tried to hold out, but the walls and city were demolished. The Turkish soldiers were allowed to riot in the city for 3 days, murdering and stealing.

SIEGE WEAPONRY

The weapons of siege warfare became very advanced during the medieval era in Europe. They included huge, sophisticated catapults which would sling darts, arrows, bolts, stones, burning tar, and dung over the city walls. Sometimes disease-ridden bodies were thrown over the walls to infect the besieged people. Large battering rams were used to knock down castle gates, and siege towers (movable towers on wheels) were used to scale the walls.

LADDERS AND WALLS

Thousands of years ago, cities started to protect themselves from murderous, thieving invaders by surrounding themselves with walls up to 20m (65ft) thick and 20m (65ft) high. The Ancient Egyptians started using long siege ladders to overcome the walls, but they soon found that their soldiers were being pushed off them, dying, or breaking their backs as a result.

STARVE OR SURRENDER

People were forced to eat cats, rats, horses, and dogs during the Siege of Colchester during the English Civil War. The Royalist army became trapped behind the town's walls in 1648 and held out for 11 weeks, while the Parliamentarian army cut off all supplies. People were forced to eat soap and candles to stay alive until the Royalists finally surrendered.

GREAT SIEGE OF GIBRALTAR

7,000 British troops almost starved to death while they defended Gibraltar, which is at the southern tip of Spain, from a relentless siege by 70,000 Spanish and French troops. The grueling siege was one of the longest in history, lasting an incredible 4 years from 1779 to 1783. The nearly dead British troops hung on during a vicious bombardment, watching more than 1,000 of their fellow soldiers die from injuries, disease, and starvation. The French and Spanish finally gave up.

AMERICAN INDEPENDENCE

The Americans crushed the British to win the War of Independence in one of the greatest sieges in history. The crucial battle occurred at Yorktown in 1781, when the American and French forces managed to block the British in the Virginia port. The Americans bombarded the British and proved to be the masters of siege warfare, capturing the outer defenses, killing 500 of the trained British soldiers, and cutting off all escape routes. The British faced complete annihilation and surrendered. Only 28 Americans were killed, while over 7,000 British soldiers were captured.

OUTNUMBERED

Another famous siege by the ruthless Ottoman Turks was the Great Siege of Malta in 1565. The Turks attacked Malta with a huge fleet of almost 200 vessels, carrying 48,000 invaders who were ready to devastate the island and slaughter the population. It looked likely that they would easily wipe out the small army of 6,000 Christian Knights Templar who were defending the island, but the Knights survived 4 months of bombardment during which 130,000 cannonballs were fired.

BLOW UP

When people burst into flames for no apparent reason at all, it's called spontaneous combustion. Most victims of spontaneous combustion are women, and tend to be overweight and to live alone. Their torso is usually burnt to a crisp, but sometimes their limbs and heads escape the flames. Weirdly, the room around is often left untouched, apart from a sooty deposit on the walls and ceiling, and sometimes a nasty-smelling yellow oil around the body.

DRESS FIRE

Phyllis Newcombe was at a dance with her boyfriend in 1938 when her dress somehow burst into flames. At first, everyone thought a lighted cigarette or match had caused the dress to burn, but tests disproved this and soon the idea of spontaneous combustion was being aired. The coroner gave a verdict of accidental death.

KROOKED!

In Charles Dickens' book *Bleak House*, one of the nastier characters, a rag-and-bone dealer called Krook, bursts into flames and dies. Many of Dickens' readers criticized this as superstitious, unscientific nonsense. Dickens said there were about 30 recorded cases of spontaneous combustion, and that in his own time working as a reporter, coroners had sometimes given it as a cause of death.

CINDER LADY

One of the most famous cases of spontaneous combustion is that of Mary Reeser of St. Petersburg, Florida. In 1951, she burst into flames while sitting in her armchair in her living room. Her body was completely charred except for one of her slippered feet, which escaped almost intact. The room was untouched by the flames apart from the corner where she was sitting. Her death remains a mystery today.

FIERY END
People used to think that spontaneous combustion was caused by an imbalance in the digestive tract. The Italian Countess Cornelia de Bandi Cesenate was feeling "dull and heavy" when she went to bed, but she was a whole lot worse when her maid found her in the morning. All that remained of her were her legs from the knees down, part of her head, three blackened fingers, and a big heap of ashes.

EARLY CASES
In 1725, Nicole Millet was found burned to death in a chair in the Lion d'Or inn in Reims, France. Her husband was accused of her murder and arrested. But the court ruled that her death was due to spontaneous combustion and he was acquitted. Fascinated by the case, Frenchman Jonas Dupont collected details of other combustion cases and, in 1763, published them in a book called *De Incendiis Corporis Humani Spontaneis* which, despite the title, caught the public imagination.

HUMAN TORCH
In the olden days, people believed that heavy drinking could cause a person to burst into flames, because of the explosive gases that would build up internally. One story was told of a 15th-century knight who'd drunk ladles of strong brandy wine. He suddenly vomited fire, set himself alight, and was burned to a crisp.

WEE CLEANSING

Inuit tribes in Alaska used to wash their bodies with their own urine. Every man had a small bucket he'd wee into. Once he'd built up a good perspiration in the sweat lodge – a communal place where men gathered to bathe – he'd pour the urine over himself, rubbing vigorously so it mixed with his body oils and worked almost like soap. Afterwards, he'd go outside and squat in the snow, pouring icy water over himself until the urine was all washed off.

IN HOT WATER

Outdoor bathing is very popular in Japan, where hot springs or "onsen" bubble up from underground. People sit in the hot springs for their health and sometimes try to achieve "yudedako," which when translated means the "boiled octopus" effect (when some kinds of octopus are boiled they turn red!). Yudedakos' skin goes puce and prune-like, and they have to be careful when they get out of the water, as they can keel over with the sudden rush of blood to the head.

GLORIOUS MUD

People often wallow around in mud to cleanse and beautify themselves. But not just any old mud. People travel a long way to find the best kind – full of minerals such as magnesium, calcium, and potassium. The Dead Sea in Jordan is an especially good place for mud. The mud there is completely black and has been famous for thousands of years. In fact, it was slathered on by Cleopatra, King Herod, and the Queen of Sheba.

HORRIBLE SCRAPERS

FINNISH FUN

In Finland, people like to sit naked and sweating in a very hot sauna, beating themselves with birch twigs. When they're sweating profusely, they race outside and roll around in the snow to cool down – then go back into the sauna and repeat the whole cycle again. Saunas are so popular in Finland that there are almost as many saunas as cars, and whole families strip off and jump in the sauna together!

SKIN SCRAPING

The Romans were very keen on going to the baths, where a slave would often "strigil" them. A strigil is a small clay or metal scythe with a curved edge which was smoothed over the skin to scrape off sweat, dirt, oil, and other gunk. Amazingly, the gruesome gray mucky stuff that came off wasn't chucked out: one Roman called Aetius Amidenus used to collect strigil scum from the baths and mix it in the beautifying creams and medications he later sold on to unsuspecting Romans. Ugh!

BLACK OOZE

In Austria, they relax in "moor mud," or peat baths. The black, fibrous peat found on the moors is made from 20,000-year-old decomposed plants which have all compacted together. Dumped in the bath, the peat makes a gloopy mineral-rich mud – the only problem is you need another bath when you get out to get rid of the sticky black bits covering you all over.

SWEATY SICKNESS

In the Mayan civilization of Mexico, people used to clean themselves in sweat houses, which they called temescals. But they also visited them whenever they were ill, to sweat out fever and pains from the body. Temescals were usually made of brick, rather like a pizza oven, with a fire in one corner and a small entrance you'd crawl through on all fours. The heat inside was intense and very dry. Once they'd sweated for a while, sick people would crawl back out and drench themselves with jugs of cold water to cool down. Then they would go back to bed exhausted.

OLiVER CROMWELL'S HEAD

When chief Puritan Oliver Cromwell died in 1658 he was buried with great ceremony. But just 2 years later, the Royalists (who did not like Cromwell) were reinstated, Cromwell's body was dug up and publicly hanged, his head was hacked off with 7 blows and paraded on a tall spike, and his headless body was chucked in a pauper's grave. For the next 300 years, Cromwell's severed head did the rounds as a circus sideshow and museum exhibit. It was secretly buried in Sidney Sussex College, Cambridge in 1960.

SARAH BERNHARDt'S LEG

When French actress Sarah Bernhardt injured her right leg, it became gangrenous and had to be amputated. She was offered a hefty sum for the rotting appendage by an impresario who wanted to display it as a medical curiosity. She was buried in Paris without her missing leg, the whereabouts of which remain unknown.

THOMAS HARDY'S HEARt

When English novelist Thomas Hardy died in 1928, people starting arguing about where his body should lie. He wanted to be buried beside his first wife in a Dorset churchyard, but his fans wanted him in Poets' Corner in London's Westminster Abbey. In the end a doctor took out Hardy's heart and buried it alongside his wife – though it's rumored the heart was eaten by his sister's cat overnight, and a pig's heart was used in its place. The rest of Hardy's body was cremated and the ashes lain in Poets' Corner.

BITS OF ST. FRANCIS XAVIER

Francis Xavier was so popular that, after he died in 1552, everybody tried to grab a bit of his body. Half of his hand is in Cochin, India; another is in Malacca, Malaysia; his right arm is in Rome; another arm bone is in Macau, China. His other remains are mostly in Goa, India.

EINSTEIN'S GRAY MATTER

Within 7 hours of his death, the brain of math genius Albert Einstein was pinched by the pathologist who did his autopsy. Dr. Thomas Harvey cut it up into 240 sections and kept it in glass preserving bottles in his house for the next 40 years. Most of the bits are now resting in jars of formaldehyde in Princeton Hospital, New Jersey, U.S.A.

LORD BYRON'S ORGANS

In 1824, English poet Lord Byron met an untimely end in Greece. His body had to be embalmed before the long sea voyage back to England. The Greek doctors saw Byron as a national hero, and decided to whip out and keep a few of his internal organs. While his body made the journey home to be buried in England, his heart and lungs are said to remain in an oil-filled jar in Missolonghi, Greece.

ST. ANTHONY'S TONGUE

St. Anthony of Padua (1195–1231) was a very eloquent preacher. Twenty-five years after he died his coffin was opened and onlookers were amazed that his tongue was still pink and glistening and had not decomposed at all. Almost 800 years on, his tongue is still on display in the Basilica of St Anthony in Padua – though it's no longer a healthy red!

THE VANISHING

The area of ocean stretching from Florida to Bermuda to Puerto Rico is known as the Bermuda Triangle. In 1945, five U.S. Avenger bombers disappeared there without trace, followed the same day by a Mariner flying boat sent to look for them. Over the next few years, more aircraft and ships vanished. Many supernatural theories have been put forward to explain these mysterious disappearances, including alien abduction or disturbances caused by the lost city of Atlantis, thought to be located below the waves.

FLYING SAUCERS

An extraordinary number of people have seen UFOs, including U.S. presidents Jimmy Carter and Ronald Reagan. But the sighting that most captured the public's imagination was that of pilot Kenneth Arnold in 1947. While flying near Mount Rainier in Washington, he said he saw a formation of nine crescent-shaped UFOs moving so fast it was like watching saucers skipping over water. His account made all the newspapers, and the phrase "flying saucer" was born.

CLOSE ENCOUNTERS

Reported sightings of aliens suggest that most are not little green men at all but 'Grays' – intelligent, gray-skinned, big-headed, bug-eyed beings, who often perform medical experiments on the humans they temporarily abduct.

LINES IN THE DESERT

In the Nazca desert in Peru, hundreds of geometric lines, alien figures, and animal shapes were made around 1,500 to 2,000 years ago. But they can only be seen from the air – so who created them? The Swiss writer Erich von Däniken believed that alien astronauts used them as runways to guide their spaceships in to land.

FRESHLY MADE PANCAKES!

COSMIC PANCAKES

In 1961, U.S. chicken farmer Joe Simonton said he was visited by a spaceship containing three tiny aliens wearing dark space suits and knitted balaclavas! Apparently, they asked him to fill up their metal jug with water and in return gave him four pancakes they'd just cooked, which he said tasted like cardboard. Then they shut the spaceship hatch, took off, and flew away.

ET IMPLANTS

People "abducted" by aliens sometimes believe they have been implanted with tiny extraterrestrial devices in their bodies. UFOlogists think these could be tracking devices, or instruments for measuring body or mind functions. More scary is the idea that the implants can manipulate people's brains and control their behavior. But, although several of these "alien" implants have been analyzed, none were found to contain otherworldly ingredients, so we're probably safe for now…

HOLLOW EARTHERS

One man didn't believe that aliens came from outer space – he thought they lived in the center of the Earth and zipped out on their spaceships through holes in the Earth's crust. John Cleves Symmes Jr. (1779–1829) wanted to dig deep holes below the polar ice caps so he could meet these kindly aliens, whom he thought were descendants of the lost civilization of Atlantis.

ALIENS CAPTURED!

The most famous UFO incident occurred at Roswell in New Mexico in 1947. After a lightning storm, William "Mac" Brazel found a large amount of strange tinfoil, rubber, and paper debris lying around. Roswell Air Force base first said this was the remains of a "flying disc," then changed its story and said it was from a weather balloon. When another witness confirmed he'd found a disc-shaped UFO and the bodies of four small, gray aliens with large heads, UFOlogists were convinced the U.S. government was covering up an alien crash landing and that some aliens, possibly still alive, had been recovered.

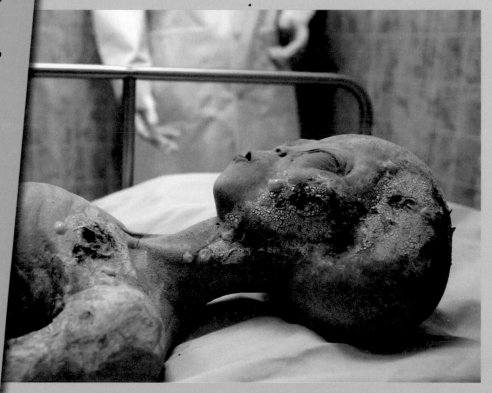

SHARP SHOOTER

Mean-eyed archerfish literally shoot their prey down with a jet of water. Using their specialized mouths, they squirt jets strong enough to bring down insects from up to 3m (10ft) above the water. The jet hits the insects, including spiders, grasshoppers, and butterflies, and they fall down so the fish can gobble them up. The archerfish's aim is amazingly accurate. It almost always hits the target first time.

CREEPY THIEF!

CORAL WARFARE

Coral may look like a stationary object on the seabed, but it is a living animal. When two corals are fighting for the same space, they use their individual sections called polyps to attack each other. The polyps squirt out their whole stomach on to their opponent, and the stomach starts to digest it to death.

KILLER NOSE

Polar bears use brute force to savagely kill animals, swiping at walruses and beluga whales with their incredibly powerful forearms. However, the bear finds its prey with a super-sensitive piece of weapons technology: its nose. A polar bear can smell a seal from 32km (20 miles) away. They can even smell them when they are under 1m (3ft) of ice. They wait for seals to surface in order to breathe. They then drag them out of the water and crush their skulls.

STOLEN ARMOR

The bizarre hermit crab has big, heavy claws which it uses as a trap-door to its shell home. That shell, however, is not its own: it uses the shell of other dead animals, carrying it on its back to protect itself. The hermit crab's biggest battle is often with another hermit crab when they both want to get their claws on the same shell. Then they start a great big claw war.

SUICIDE BEES

The honey bee is one of the animal kingdom's most extreme fighters, because it gives up its own life when it uses its weapon. The bee has a barbed sting at the end of its abdomen, which it will use if it thinks its hive is under threat. When a mammal is stung, the barb stays in the skin and part of the bee's abdomen is ripped off when it flies away, ensuring its own certain death.

BLOOD SQUIRTER

The horned lizard, also called the horned toad, tries to put off predators by looking fierce, with sharp spines all over its back and horns on its head. If that does not work, it uses a horrible defense system. The lizard is able to shoot blood from the corner of its eyes for a distance up to 1.5m (5ft). The blood-squirt confuses the predator and also tastes foul, so the attacker usually decides to find its lunch elsewhere.

UGH! WHEN ANGRY, LLAMAS … DIFFERENT TYPES OF … SMELLING SALIVA … …ONENTS.

SPIKY DEFENSE

Even really fierce predators such as lions will run away from an angry porcupine. These weird rodents, which can grow up to 85cm (33in) long, are covered with ultra-sharp, spiky quills which form a great defense system. If a lion tries to grab a porcupine, it will get a pawful of painful needles. Porcupines can also shake their quills off their backs to create a mass attack of sharp needles.

STINK FIGHTS

The lemur, which is a monkey-like animal only found on the Pacific island of Madagascar, will happily have a stink fight in an attempt to beat an opponent. The ring-tailed lemur secretes smelly liquids into its tail and then waves its tail in the face of male rivals.

OFF WITH THE HAND!!!

BRAVEST CUT

Sometimes people are so brave that they cut off their own limbs in order to save their life. Aron Ralston was hiking by himself in a canyon in Utah, U.S.A., when a boulder fell on his arm and pinned him to the ground. After 5 days, Ralston decided that sawing his arm off was the only way to escape. While staggering from the canyon he was found by some walkers who called the rescue services and saved his life.

LEG-SAVING TREATMENT

In 1865, a young boy called James Greenlees was run over by a cart and his leg was badly broken with the bones sticking through the skin. Usually open wounds became infected, so the person would lose their limb or even die. But British surgeon Joseph Lister applied the antiseptic carbolic acid to young James's wound before splinting it. Six weeks later, the boy walked out of the hospital healed, thanks to the bacteria-killing properties of the antiseptic.

MILITARY WOUNDS

Once soldiers started using muskets instead of swords and lances, war wounds became very gruesome. Musket balls caused a lot of damage to flesh and bone, and wounds quickly became infected. It's thought that many more soldiers died from infected wounds than in battle itself. In the terrible trenches of World War I, soldiers' wounds were even more horrendous, because they became contaminated with the bacteria that causes deadly gangrene and tetanus. Surgeons had to cut away all the dead flesh and pack the wound with gauze for 5 days, before then sewing it up.

CAREER AMPUTATION

In 2002, Australian football player Daniel Chick decided to have his ring finger amputated so he could continue playing professionally. It used to cause him grief – during matches, he'd often dislocate it, then have to miss the next few games because he was injured. So he decided to chop it off once and for all.

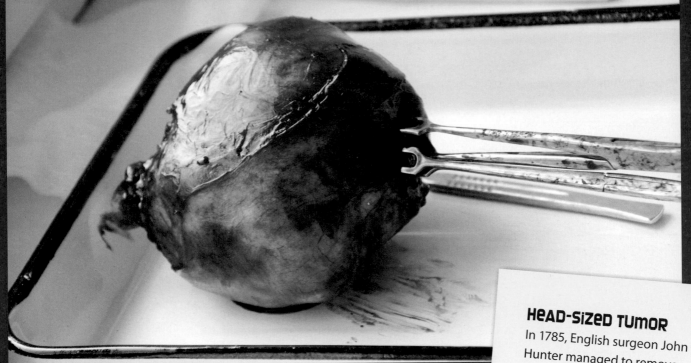

HEAD-SIZED TUMOR

In 1785, English surgeon John Hunter managed to remove an enormous tumor attached to the neck of a man called John Burley. It took 25 minutes to cut out the tumor, which was twice the size of Burley's head and weighed 4kg (9lb). The man survived, and John Hunter kept the tumor in his huge anatomical collection for many years.

SCREAM AND BEAR IT

Amputations used to be carried out without any kind of painkillers – though some people were lucky enough to be given strong liquor or laudanum, a mixture of opium in alcohol, to dull the agony. It wasn't until 1812 that Baron *Dominique-Jean* Larrey, Napoleon's chief surgeon, started freezing limbs with ice before amputating them. This worked like a local anesthetic, so people felt much less pain.

TOUGH ANIMAL

Sula, a Collie-cross dog in Manitoba, Canada, got caught in a trap set for coyotes – and was so desperate that she chewed her front leg off to escape. She managed to hobble home on three legs, and is now doing very well.

PHANTOM LIMBS

Many amputees say they can still "feel" the body part that is no longer there. It itches, tingles, aches or feels stiff, hot or cold, and sometimes they even feel it "moving" with the rest of the body. Phantom limb syndrome is thought to be caused by damaged nerve endings or altered activity in the brain.

SCARED SPIDERS

Spiders have their own gruesome enemies, including mud daubers. This type of wasp likes to capture spiders, including young black widows. It seals the spider in a nest cell, along with one of its own eggs, which grows into larva while feeding on the spider.

BEWARE THE FEMALE

It is usually female spiders rather than males that are the scariest. They are often larger and more vicious, and give the males a very hard time. In some species, male spiders try to please females by bringing them a meal of a tasty insect. If the meal is not good enough, the female will eat the male instead.

AMERICA'S MOST DANGEROUS

The most frightening spider found in the United States is the southern black widow, which lives in the southeastern states. The female is much deadlier than the male. She is glossy black with red markings on her underside, and sometimes eats her mate, which is how the species earned its name. About 2,500 black widow bites on humans are reported every year.

VENOMOUS CREATURE

DEADLY AUSSIE

One of the deadliest spiders in Australia is the redback spider. Its venom even causes pain in mammals as large as humans. The female spider, which has a red stripe on a black body, is particularly nasty to the male. Quite often, she eats it while they are mating, so that she will have enough food to feed her young.

HAIRY DEFENSE

Some spiders, including tarantulas, are covered with hairs which they use as a weapon. They kick the hairs from their abdomen towards a possible attacker. The hairs get stuck in the animal's skin and eyes, which become really irritated, thereby distracting the attacker.

THE NASTY MALE

The Australian funnel-web spider is one of the most dangerous species in the world, but unusually it is the male, not the female, which is the real killer. Over the last 100 years, 26 human deaths have been reported as a result of funnel-web spider bites. In every case where the sex of the spider has been known, it has been male.

BIG TARANTULA

The biggest spider in the world is the goliath birdeater spider. As the name suggests, it is partial to snacking on a whole bird, having killed it with venom from its fangs. It also eats rodents, bats, and snakes. It is a type of tarantula and can have a huge legspan up to 25cm (11in).

SCORPION STINGER

About 1,000 people are killed by scorpions every year. They sting with their tails, which have a sharp barb on the end that injects the victim with venom. The venom paralyzes or kills the victim, depending on their size. A scorpion will go mad and sting itself to death if you put alcohol on its back.

SPOOKY GIRL STORY

A beautiful girl in a floaty evening gown is sometimes seen hitching a ride on a busy road. When someone picks her up, she says her name is Lydia, and that she's had car trouble coming home from a party. She always chats away while being driven home, but as soon as the car stops outside her house, she vanishes. When the driver asks inside, they're told Lydia was killed many years before in a dreadful car crash on her way home from her 21st birthday party.

MYTH OR TRUTH?

An urban myth or legend is a story that people think is true, even though it is almost definitely not. These events have usually happened to the friend of a friend, and are so horrifying or scary or mysterious that people somehow believe they really occurred. Urban myths have been around forever. In the olden days, people thought the world was round and sailors could fall off the end of it in a boat. One modern urban myth is that alligators are living in New York City's sewers, and occasionally pop out to bite someone's leg off or drag them down through manholes.

SWALLOW THIS!

A tall woman accidentally swallowed a tadpole when she was swimming in a river. Three months later, while undergoing an operation, it's said that a frog jumped out of her stomach.

SHAGGY DOG TALE

When a woman returns home after an evening out with friends, she's said to find her Doberman in the hall, choking. She rushes the dog to the veterinarian who immediately performs an emergency operation to open its windpipe – and finds 3 severed fingers there. The woman calls the police who race to her home and find a burglar with a severed hand, who's passed out in her bedroom closet from losing so much blood.

KIDNEY HEIST LEGEND

A man was said to be on a business trip alone in Eastern Europe when he went for a drink in a local cafe. When he woke up next morning, he found himself in a bath of ice in an unfamiliar hotel room, with a terrible pain in his back. In the hospital emergency room, the doctors told him that his right kidney had been surgically removed, presumably by a professional gang who wanted to sell it for a fortune on the black market.

SPIDER CYST MYTH

A young woman was said to be sunbathing on a tropical beach when she felt an insect running across her face. She quickly brushed it off, and thought nothing more of it. A week later, she was putting on her make-up when she noticed a small hard cyst-like lump on her cheek. Three days later, the lump had grown red and inflamed and was ready to pop. She squeezed it – and 50 or more baby spiders came pouring out of the egg sac cyst, which had been incubating under her skin.

JERSEY DEVIL

This two-legged winged creature with hooves is said to inhabit the Pine Barrens area of New Jersey, U.S.A. It's thought to be the 13th child of an 18th-century witch, who decided she didn't want it. It's been "sighted" many times over the past 200 years, and is sometimes heard rampaging through the countryside emitting bloodcurdling shrieks.

BEETLE BRAIN

In 19th-century Yugoslavia and Albania, it was said that the apprentice of the chief physician, while hiding behind a curtain, saw the esteemed doctor make a big hole in the forehead of the Czar's daughter. He then removed a beetle from her brain.

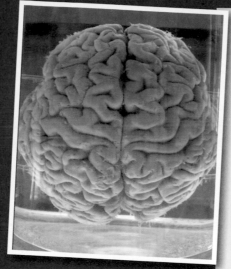

BiG BRAiN

The biggest brain recorded in the 19th century was not that of a genius – but a common criminal. American Edward Rulloff spent most of his life in jail, but he was always regarded as a "criminal of superior intelligence" because of his quick mind and interest in learning new things. When he was hanged for murder in 1871, Professor Burt Green Wilder of Cornell University extracted and weighed his brain – and was amazed to find it was the largest the world had ever known. Rulloff's brain is still kept in a jar of formaldehyde in the Wilder Brain Collection at Cornell.

ANiMAL BALLOONS

The Aztecs used to make animal balloons out of cats' stomachs and bowels. They'd clean them, blow them up, then twist them into dog and donkey shapes, which they'd offer as sacrifices to their gods.

YUK!

IN WORLD WAR II, U.S. ARMY SURGEON DWIGHT HARKEN USED TO PULL SHRAPNEL OUT OF SOLDIERS' STILL-BEATING HEARTS WITH HIS FINGERS.

TOUGH LIVER

Even when badly damaged, internal organs can renew themselves. U.S. soldier F. A. Bernard of the 37th Wisconsin Regiment was shot in 1864. The bullet cut a hole through his liver, winged his lung and sliced a bit off his gall bladder, causing greeny-yellow, ghastly smelling bile to pour out of the hole in his side. He vomited for the first 24 hours and hiccoughed for the next – which used to be thought a sign of approaching death. But on the 10th day, Mr. Bernard started to get better, and his internal organs repaired themselves so well that he was still alive 17 years later.

UNDER THE SKIN

In the 1970s, German anatomist Dr. Gunther von Hagens invented a way of preserving bodies and organs with a special plastic. It means they last for years without decaying or smelling, yet still retain their "living" appearance. He exhibits his "plastinated" dead bodies – donated by their owners while they were still alive – in shows that tour the world. He also once carried out a medical examination of a 72-year-old man's body for television. He opened the man's chest, pulled out his lungs and heart, cut off his head and displayed his brain. This was the first public autopsy in Britain for 170 years and it caused an uproar.

HOLE IN THE HEAD

In 1848, Phineas Gage was working as the foreman of a road-building team in Vermont, U.S.A. There was an explosion and his long, iron tamping rod was pushed upward through his cheek and brain and out of the top of his head with such force it landed 25m (80ft) away. He was left with a hole right through his face and in the frontal lobes of his brain – doctors said that a teacupful of his brain landed on the floor after the injury. Amazingly, Mr. Gage survived for 12 years after the gruesome accident, though his personality was said to have changed dramatically.

FORK STABS LUNG!

An American man from North Carolina spent 2 years suffering from coughing, exhaustion, and bouts of pneumonia. Nobody could find out what was wrong with him – until eventually it was discovered he had a plastic fork prong 2.5cm (1in) long stuck in his lung! When doctors operated to remove the fork, they found the logo of a fast-food chain still imprinted on it.

SPOT THE PLOP

In Ystad in Sweden every year they play a game of Cow Bingo. A field is marked off into 81 squares and people place bets on which square a wandering cow will drop a pat on first. Any liquid or runny stuff is not considered – only solid poop counts!

MUD WRESTLING

The mucky sport of mud wrestling is popular all over the world. In India, the tradition is called Kushti and is over 3,000 years old. Kushti wrestlers live together under strict rules and train for hours every day. They wrestle in pits, where the clay has been mixed with ghee (clarified butter) to make it thicker and stickier. In other countries, people wrestle covered in oil, Jell-O, mashed potatoes, baked beans, and even creamed corn.

DON'T BREATHE DEEPLY!

Bog snorkeling is one of the world's grubbiest sports. Competitors have to propel themselves 120m (400ft) up and down the smelly, dirty, cold waters of a peat bog trench wearing a swimsuit and snorkeling mask (wetsuit is optional), relying on flipper power alone. The fastest person is the winner, provided they can survive immersion in the stinky brown stuff for long enough to complete the course.

TOE-WRESTLING

This smelly sport involves 2 bare-footed people on a "toedium" trying to wrestle each other's foot to the ground. They interlock their (hopefully clean) big toes and use ankle strength to push their opponent's foot over. To win, they have to "pin," or hold, the opposition's foot down for 3 seconds – and try not to catch any nasty foot infections in the process!

WiFE-CARRYiNG

The strongman sport of wife-carrying originated in Finland, but is now popular round the world. Men carry their wives (or any woman over 18) over a grass, sand, and gravel obstacle course with 2 log hurdles to climb over and one water hole to wade through. The women are carried by piggyback, on shoulders or clamped upside down on the man's back. It can be gruesomely dangerous, with slipped discs, hernias, broken legs, arm fractures, and spinal damage regularly reported. The wives don't get off lightly either: they're sometimes dropped on their heads.

CHARMiNG WORMS

Could you entice 567 wriggly worms out of the ground in half an hour? That's how many Sophie Smith and her dad Matt managed to catch in the World Worm Charming Champions of 2009. Competitors have half an hour to entice as many worms out of the ground as they can. They work in pairs, one person "twanging" the tines of a garden fork buried a few centimeters in the ground, while the other picks off the little worms that come to the surface thinking food is around. The rules of the competition, held since 1980 in Cheshire, England, state that cutting worms in half to double your score is definitely not allowed!

WiLD POLO

Buzkashi is an Afghan game played on horseback – but instead of a ball it's played with a dead calf. The calf is decapitated, its legs are cut off at the knees, its entrails are taken out and the cavity filled with sand to make it heavier. Players have to grab the calf and carry it while galloping at full tilt across the pitch. To score a goal, they have to toss the calf into a scoring area at the other end of the pitch. It's a rough, tough game in which the riders use whips and pull the other team off their horses to stop them scoring.

HAIRIEST OF ALL

Some people's faces and bodies are completely covered with thick hair, almost like a wolf's. This is called hypertrichosis and it's an extremely rare genetic condition. One of the first recorded cases was Petrus Gonzales in the mid-16th century. People were so astounded by his hairiness that, as an infant, he was taken from his home in the Canary Islands to the court of King Henri II of France. His hairy face and body, combined with the excellent education and manners he received at court, caused such a sensation that he became famous throughout Europe.

SMELLY WIG

HAIR Detectives

By analyzing a person's hair, you can tell a lot about them, including what substances have passed through their body, and whether they've been poisoned or exposed to heavy metals. From hair samples taken long ago, you can find out more about how people died. Emperor Napoleon of France was thought to have been poisoned by the arsenic that was in his green wallpaper. But recent tests on his hair have proved that the levels of arsenic in his body were normal for his time.

EAR HAIR TRIUMPH

Radhakant Bajpai from Uttar Pradesh in India has so much hair sprouting from his ears that he can tie it into two ponytails. Each lughole tuft has reached an astonishing 13.2cm (5.19in) in length. He's so proud of his ear hair that he washes it with special shampoo!

PERFUMED WIGS

Priests and well-born Ancient Egyptians used to believe hair was unclean. They meticulously removed it from everywhere on their body, and cropped or shaved their heads, too. But they then wore elaborate curly and perfumed wigs, often made of human hair, on top of their heads.

GROWTH RATES

Did you know that hair on different areas of the body grows at very different rates? In a typical month, mustaches and beards grow by about 1.2cm; head hair by 1cm; body hair by 0.8cm; and eyebrows by 0.45cm.

HAIRY HUMANS

Surprisingly, most humans have much more hair than gorillas, apes and orang-utans – it's just that it is finer and shorter so you don't notice it as much. A human being has about 20 million hairs on the body and head. In prehistoric days, these hairs were much thicker so people looked more apelike than now – they needed the hairy covering to keep warm.

SELF-CLEANING HAIR

Dogs and cats don't wash their hair, and it stays fluffy and soft. Amazingly, human hair is self-cleaning too. People who stop washing their hair find that after about a month, it becomes glossy, clean and sweet-smelling. It's thought that the chemicals in shampoos and other hair products upset hair's natural oil balance. But just like a dog having a dunk in the river, humans have to give their hair a rinse with water to get the dirt out.

VERMIN WIGS

In the 18th century, rich people wore wigs made out of horsehair which was curled and waved, and then covered with white powder. Even men wore wigs, because they would shave off all their real hair to get rid of lice. The wigs were often infested with bugs, though, and sometimes small rodents would nest in them.

BURKE AND HARE

William Burke and William Hare of Edinburgh, Scotland, became the most famous body snatchers of all time. They could not be bothered with all that digging, though. Their first victim died of natural causes. They took his body to an anatomy lecturer called Dr. Robert Knox, who paid them very well. From then on they started suffocating their victims, killing 16. After they were arrested, Burke was hanged and his body was dissected at Edinburgh Medical College in 1829.

SELLING CORPSES

Body snatching usually involved stealing human corpses from graveyards or tombs. The main reason for body snatching was to sell the corpses to doctors lecturing in anatomy, dissection, or surgery in medical schools. Sometimes, bodies were also plundered from ancient tombs, such as those of the Egyptian pharaohs.

DEATHLY TECHNIQUES

To begin with, the body snatchers used to dig down through the earth to the head of the coffin, break open the top, and drag the body up with a rope. So many graves were robbed that friends and family of the dead started to carefully watch over the body before it was buried, and then watch over the grave after the funeral. Some body snatchers changed tactics: they would tunnel their way to the coffin and drag the body back with them. The grave-watchers never knew the body had gone.

A BRITISH HABIT

Body snatching was very common in Britain. Before a change in the law in 1832, the only dead bodies that could legally be used for medical study were the corpses of criminals who had been condemned to death. At the beginning of the 19th century, this only provided 50 bodies a year, but the medical schools needed 10 times that number. As a result, the medical schools paid people to steal fresh dead bodies for them. The thieves became known as "resurrection men."

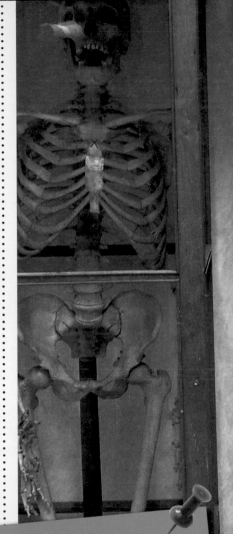

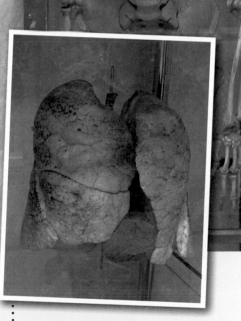

DIGGING DOCTORS

Body snatchers were also hard at work in America in the 18th and 19th centuries. Even doctors themselves became involved in the process. In 1769, Dr. John Collins Warren and his colleagues founded a secret group called the Spunkers. The gruesome group would dig up bodies from graves, cut them up, and study them.

FINAL SNATCH

In London in 1831, body snatchers John Bishop and Thomas Williams killed a 14-year-old boy and sold his body to a doctor. However, when the doctor examined the body, he realized the boy had been murdered. Bishop and Williams were executed and the law was finally changed to give doctors legal access to unclaimed corpses, which put an end to the body snatchers' profession in England.

TAKEN FOR MUSEUMS

The Pitt-Rivers Museum in Oxford, England, specializes in ancient human remains from around the world. It has 2,000 objects that are either human remains or have been made out of human remains, including mummies, shrunken skulls, and bracelets made from human hair. Some of the objects were originally stolen from burial sites, but now the museum tries to display them with respect.

DOCTORS' RIOT

In April 1788, the people of New York decided that they had had enough of people stealing corpses from graves for doctors to cut them up in anatomy lessons. A huge frenzied mob stormed a hospital in what became America's first riot. They were baying for blood and searched for doctors to lynch while completely destroying the inside of the hospital. The doctors jumped out windows and ran for their lives.

ANIMALS SWALLOWED WHOLE

Pythons can grow up to 10.5m (35ft) long and need some big meals. They ambush their victims and suffocate them to death by constricting their ribs. Then they swallow their prey, head first. This is no mean feat as their prey includes pigs, deer, and even gazelles. It can take weeks for a python to digest a really large animal. There are about 3,000 pythons in Florida, but most of them do not eat anything larger than a cat.

THE REAL GLUTTON

The wolverine is so greedy it is simply called "glutton" or "fat belly" in many parts of Europe. With powerful jaws, lethal claws and tough skin, this predator will take on absolutely anyone, even animals that are many times bigger, such as brown bears. They often inhabit the same territory as wolves, feeding on the carrion left behind. Once it finds a meal, a bingeing wolverine will defend it aggressively. Wolverines also give off a disgusting smell, which has led to its other nickname, "skunk bear."

BONE EATER

The Tasmanian devil, which lives on the island of Tasmania in Australia, is a ferocious feeder. It is only the size of a small to medium dog, but it has the strongest bite of all mammals in the animal kingdom. It can devour up to 40% of its own body weight in just 30 minutes, eating every scrap of its prey including its fur and bones. It will eat anything it can get its hands on, including small kangaroos, wombats, fish, and rotting corpses.

LITTLE GOBBLER

The tiny hummingbird might look delicate but don't be fooled. It will eat up to 5 times its own body weight in nectar every single day, while also devouring side dishes of insects and spiders. The birds need to feed every 10 minutes because they beat their wings so incredibly fast that they use up all the energy from their food almost as soon as they've eaten it.

BUTCHER BIRD

The gluttonous shrike looks quite cute, but it's a vicious, territorial bird with a sharp curved beak. Shrikes are known for their habit of catching insects, small birds, or mammals and impaling their bodies on thorns. They then rip up the flesh into conveniently sized portions to tuck into later on. Not surprisingly, the shrike goes by the nickname of "butcher bird."

FAT SEAL

Big, blubbery male elephant seals are up to 6 times larger than females. The elephant seal gets its name from its rather ugly snout, and grows to a massive length of 5m (16ft), weighing up to 2,700kg (6,000lb). The largest recorded elephant seal measured nearly 7m (23ft) snout to tail. Much of that bulk is blubber, gained from eating skates, eels, octopuses, and small sharks. They will even devour penguins.

HUNGRY FROG

The grub-loving Argentine horned frog will try to eat absolutely anything that comes near it – lizards, rodents, even humans – even if it gets suffocated in the process! It is also known as the Argentine wide-mouthed frog because its massive mouth takes up almost half its body. It sits motionless until something enters its strike range, and then it pounces.

COW BRAIN FEAST

Takeru Kobayashi is obsessed with breaking gross eating records, but his most disgusting yet is wolfing 8kg (17.7lb) of slimy cow brains in just 15 minutes. In Nathan's Hot Dog Eating Contest, held in Coney Island every year and which he won 6 years in a row, he once forced down 64.5 frankfurters and their buns. He wiggles his body while he eats in the belief that this helps him to swallow such a humungous amount of food more quickly.

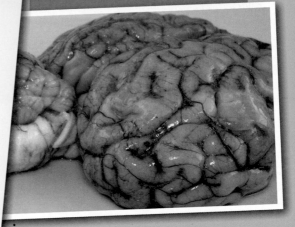

NETTLE CHAMP

Simon Sleigh from Hawkchurch, England, is a 3 times winner of the World Stinging Nettle Eating Championships. In 2002, he managed to eat an astonishing 23m (76ft) of nettles in just 1 hour. At the Championships, contestants are given long, specially grown stalks of nettles with the leaves still attached, which they have to strip off and eat as fast as they can.

BIG MAC MAN

Donald Gorske has eaten over 23,000 Big Macs in one of the biggest food addictions of all time. The man from Font du Lac in Wisconsin didn't eat all those burgers in one massive, gross sitting but over the course of his lifetime. He first discovered the burgers in 1972 and liked them so much he ate 9 on the first day. Big Macs now make up 90% of his diet and he keeps an emergency hoard in his freezer to ensure he can have at least one every day, even if his favorite restaurant is shut.

MR. MANGETOUT

The French entertainer Mr. Mangetout (which means "eats everything" in French) has eaten television sets, bicycles, and even a Cessna 150 aircraft on stage – and is alive to tell the tale. When doctors examined Michel Lotito to see why he didn't suffer any gruesome after-effects from his metal-eating adventures, they found his stomach lining was twice as thick as normal, which must have protected him a bit.

BURGER GROSS-OUT

American Sean Durnal stuffed an amazing, indigestion-inducing, 5 quarter-pound hamburgers with cheese into his mouth in just 3 minutes. The man from Ford Scott in Kansas was 17 when he achieved the stomach-churning record in 2008. He had to swallow every single scrap within the time limit. The previous record had been 4 quarter pounders in 3 minutes.

COCKROACH CRUNCHER

Just the thought of having a cockroach inside their mouth would make some people feel ill, but Ken Edwards got his own back on the disgusting, scuttling creatures when he ate 36 of them in just 1 minute. On a television show in London, 2001, he crunched his way through one cockroach after another without stopping. Mr. Edwards is used to dealing with revolting animals: he used to be a rat-catcher.

YUK!

THE COMPETITIVE EATER SONYA THOMAS ONCE ATE 48 SLIMY, SLIPPERY RAW OYSTERS IN JUST 10 MINUTES.

PIZZA SUCKER

A New Zealander called Josh Anderson once ate a whole 12-inch pizza in just 1 minute 45 seconds. He virtually sucked the pizza down rather than chewing it properly. Maybe he should have ordered a bigger pizza if he was that hungry. He broke the record for quickest pizza eating in Wellington, New Zealand, in 2008.

THE LEMON EATER

Eating a single slice of lemon is enough to make most people wince at its acid sharpness, but Gekidan Hitori managed to peel and eat 3 whole lemons in just 1 minute 33 seconds. He achieved the peculiar feat on 28 April 2008 in Tokyo in Japan.

GRIM TATTOOS

In 17th-century Japan, criminals who committed serious offenses were tattooed on the face or forearms so they could be easily identified. The tattoos were of crosses, double lines, circles, bars or symbols, sometimes showing where the crime had been committed. Tattooing was considered a very severe punishment: anyone wearing one of these tattoos would be rejected by their family and certainly avoided by everyone else.

HANGED, DRAWN, AND QUARTERED

One of the most spectacularly gruesome punishments in medieval times was for high treason, or plotting crimes against the ruler or king. The criminal would be dragged on a wooden frame to a public place of execution, and hanged until almost dead. The victim was then cut down, disemboweled or his insides "drawn" out, and beheaded. His body was cut into 4 pieces, called "quartering." The head and body parts would often be displayed on sticks to deter anyone with anti-royal ideas. Different countries had different quartering techniques. In Russia, all 4 limbs were cut off before the victim was beheaded.

GUM LITTERING

Since 1992, it has been illegal to take chewing gum into Singapore, even for personal use. Before the ban, the city-state was bedevilled by chewing gum vandals who used to stick "dead" or used gum on train door sensors to stop them shutting, in car and door locks, and letterboxes to cause havoc, and of course dropped it on the pavement where it had to be cleaned off at great expense. The only kind of gum you'll see someone in Singapore chewing is "medicinal" gum for tooth decay.

IN THE STOCKS

During medieval times, people were often put in the stocks or pillory when they committed a crime. These were wooden frames with holes for their hands and feet (stocks) or neck and hands (pillory) which were locked shut so that it was impossible for the person to escape. The stocks were usually built on the village green so crowds of people could come and jeer at the prisoner, whip their feet, spit on them, throw stones and rotten food at them, and sometimes even beat them up.

LOST HANDS

In some countries today pickpockets and those caught stealing will still be punished by having a hand chopped.

ANTI-GAROTTING SOCIETIES

In 1860s' London, criminals began "garotting" their victims in dark alleyways. A thief would grab a victim round the neck and choke him while his accomplices stole from his pockets. There was such an outcry at these violent attacks that anti-garotting societies were formed to hunt down offenders, and one magazine jokingly featured spiked steel collars to protect citizens from the threat! Garotting was taken so seriously that in 1863 the law was changed so that anyone caught doing it was flogged as well as imprisoned for their crime.

HANGING OFFENSES

It is a gruesome fact that in Britain in 1822, the death penalty was handed out for any one of 222 very minor crimes. These included stealing bread, shoplifting, cutting down a tree, slitting the nose, poaching a rabbit, or blacking the face to commit burglary. In the 10 years to 1789, there were over 530 hangings in the London area alone – that's about one a week! There was such an outrage about people hanging for such trivial crimes that, in 1823, Sir Robert Peel reduced the number of capital offenses by 100.

STICKY FLYPAPER

There are over 100 types of flypaper traps, which are plants with a killing mechanism just like flypaper. These include butterworts, which have mucous droplets that look like water on their leaves. Insects are tricked into landing on the leaf to have a drink, but their feet become stuck in the mucus. The plant then consumes the struggling, trapped insect.

VERY TALL AND SMELLY

The kapok tree is one of the largest plants on Earth, but it is also one of the smelliest. Located in the Amazonian rainforest and Southeast Asia, it can grow up to 61m (200ft) high at a staggering rate of 4m (13ft) a year. The tree's white and pink flowers smell disgustingly vile to humans, but bats like the odor. They gorge themselves on the flowers' nectar and become covered in the tree's pollen in the process, which helps the kapok to fertilize its seeds over a wide area.

Bean Poison

The castor bean, which is used to make castor oil, is lethal. It is the most poisonous plant in the world because it contains deadly ricin. Ricin causes a burning sensation in the mouth and throat, followed by dehydration and internal bleeding, and if untreated will lead to death. Just 4 to 8 beans are enough to kill an adult. In order to make castor oil, which is used in food, the ricin is removed by filtering.

DEADLY NIGHTSHADE

One of the most poisonous plants is deadly nightshade, also known as Atropa belladonna, a name which implies that death is decided by a beautiful lady. The killer plant's leaves and berries are highly toxic: 10 to 20 berries can kill an adult, and just a couple can kill a small child.

Killer Tree

The strangler fig is a murderer, killing other trees. Its seeds are deposited in the rooftops of the tropical rainforests by birds and monkeys that have eaten figs. The seeds fall into the branch crevices of a tree and they start to grow roots downward, wrapping around the host tree and slowly strangling the life out of it. The host tree eventually suffocates and dies.

Venus Flytrap

The Venus flytrap is the best-known carnivorous plant in the world. It catches and eats insects and spiders using a vicious trap made out of hinged lobes with spikes on the end and tiny hairs in the middle. When an insect lands on the lobes and disturbs the hairs, the lobes suddenly shut in just 0.1 seconds. The Venus flytrap then begins to digest the insect. It is native only to North and South Carolina, but has become a popular plant all over the world.

THE KILLER QUEEN

Catherine de Medici took her family's murderous expertise to France when she married the future King Henry II. A Catholic, she was very involved in political intrigue against the Protestant Huguenots. She is believed to have killed the Protestant Queen of Navarre in 1572 by poisoning the inside of her gloves. Catherine had a secret passage to the laboratory of her own scientist, who concocted poisonous potions as well as perfumes.

THE MEDICIS

The Medici family was the wealthiest family in Europe and one of the most influential in Italy from the 15th to the 18th centuries. The reason why they were so successful was that they were very good at getting rid of their rivals, by any means. In late 15th- and 16th-century Italy, the Borgias were even worse in their pursuit of power. They were accused of theft, rape, incest, and murder, especially by poison.

FAMILY MURDERS

The Medicis had many enemies but the people they had to beware of the most were members of their own family. They constantly fought each other for ultimate wealth and power. Lorenzino de Medici killed his cousin Alessandro, the Duke of Florence, in 1537. He then ran away to Venice, where he gained the nickname Lorenzaccio, "Bad Lorenzo," for decapitating statues. In the end, he was assassinated on the orders of his relative, Cosimo de Medici.

MONKEY BUSINESS

People in Renaissance Italy loved playing gruesome practical jokes on each other. In 1537, when Florentine banker Francesco del Nero was in jail for tax fraud, his enemies decided to let a Barbary ape into his dungeon in the dead of night. Coming out of sleep, del Nero was horrified at the hairy creature scratching his skin and tugging at his hair. He was convinced he'd been transported to Hell and this was a devil tormenting him, and ran around screaming in abject horror. His terror so amused his "friends" that they wrote a sonnet about it.

CESARE THE STRANGLER

For political reasons, Cesare Borgia murdered his sister's lover and then attacked her second husband, Alfonso V of Aragon, in 1500. First of all, his henchmen severely beat up Alfonso as he was out walking in Rome. Cesare then took matters into his own hands. He managed to get into the bedroom where his brother-in-law was recovering and strangle him.

POISONED DRINK

Lucrezia Borgia, who was rumored to have had a child with her own brother Cesare, became the most infamous of the Borgia murderers. She was said to have had a hollow ring which she would fill with poison. If she did not like somebody, she would secretly empty the contents of her ring into their drink.

POPE'S KIDS

Popes are not meant to get married or have children, but Rodrigo Borgia, who became Pope Alexander VI in 1492, had at least 8 children including Cesare and Lucrezia Borgia, both of whom are suspected of becoming serial killers. One of Cesare's first evil acts was to kill his own older brother, Giovanni, and throw his body in the River Tiber in Rome.

FATAL REVENGE

When the very unpleasant Francesco de Medici wanted to marry his mistress Bianca, he decided to kill both his own wife and Bianca's husband. Francesco and Bianca were then free to remarry and thought that they would live happily ever after. However, they were both poisoned by one of their many enemies on the same day in 1587.

ARSENIC FOR THEM

The philosophers Pico della Mirandola and Angelo Poliziano died mysteriously within weeks of each other in 1494, aged 30 and 40. Their bodies were exhumed in 2007, and studied. Forensic tests have revealed the two probably died of horrific arsenic poisoning.

VIRAL INVADERS

Although bacteria are tiny, viruses are about 100 times tinier! They can't survive for too long on their own, so they invade the cells of other creatures instead. They persuade their hosts to churn out replicas of themselves – just like a virus factory. Viruses can't easily be killed, which makes them very dangerous. They cause some of the world's nastiest diseases.

MARTIAN MICROBES

Is there life on Mars? Scientists think that prokaryotes might exist on other planets. These are the very simplest type of bacteria. They are just a bit of DNA (biological information) floating in a cell. That's it! They've been around for about 3 billion years and are so tough that they can live anywhere – under glaciers, miles beneath rock, on the sea floor, and perhaps even in outer space!

IT'S A MICROBE WORLD!

Microbes are everywhere – on every surface you touch, inside every living being, in soil, water, and air. There are trillions and trillions and trillions more of them than of any other living being on Earth. But the amazing thing is that we can't see them – and until the invention of the microscope, nobody was sure they existed. Microbes include bacteria, viruses, and some microscopic plants, fungi, and animals such as plankton and amoeba. Microbes are often useful, like the bacterial yeast that makes bread rise. But some are very dangerous.

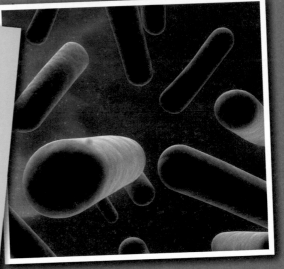

HOW VIRUSES SPREAD...

The norovirus, or winter vomiting bug, makes you projectile vomit – one minute you feel fine and the next the walls opposite are covered with sick! This forceful vomiting infects a "blast zone" of up to 6m (20ft) with the tiny bits of virus. They fly through the air, landing on furniture, curtains, carpets, and walls – where they happily live for days. The next person in the room only needs to take in 10-100 of them to become ill, and so the viral cycle carries on…

Mini-mites

Did you know that tiny mites live in the roots of your eyelashes? They're so small you can't see them, but they look like mini-worms with front claws. They push their head into the hole where the hair grows, and leave their bottom halves waggling out. They feed on the dead skin and oily stuff they find in there. Luckily, they don't produce any bodily wastes, so your eyelashes are not covered in mite poo!

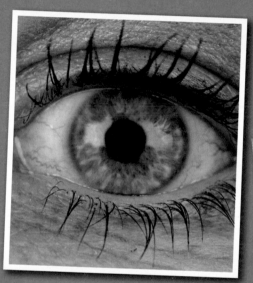

BACTERIAL CLEAN-UP

Often, bacteria do very good things – like helping us make bread, wine, yogurt, and cheese. They live in our gut and help us process food. Antibiotics and other medicines are made from them. But now scientists are using bacteria to clean up our polluted environment, too. Bacteria can remove carbon dioxide from the atmosphere, break down toxic waste, and even disperse oil spills.

OOZING AMOEBAS

Amoebas can be small or large, but the one thing they all do is ooze! They are single-celled creatures, shapeless, and jelly-like, and they're always on the hunt for food. They "chase" their prey by extending a bit of their body forward – then the rest of them oozes into it behind. When they find something tasty like bacteria or algae, they engulf it, rather like The Blob (see p74).

WOW!

WEIRD EXTINCT ANIMALS

SABER-TOOTHED TIGER

A cat as big as a bear, with canine teeth measuring 28cm (11in), the smilodon could open its jaws twice as wide as a lion and even rip apart a mammoth! This vicious, smiling, killer cat lived in North and South America until 12,000 years ago. It weighed up to a massive 400kg (880lb), and its stabbing teeth gave it the nickname "saber-toothed tiger."

MONSTER BIRD

The terrifying Phorusrhacos, nicknamed "Terror Bird," was a flightless monster 2.5m (8ft) tall and weighing 130kg (280lb). Its enormous head had a huge hooked beak with which it held its prey, repeatedly smashing it on the ground, while its unused feathers had claws shaped like meat hooks. It lived in the Americas until 15,000 years ago.

DEAD AS A DODO

The most famous extinct animal in history, the dodo gave rise to the saying "Dead as a dodo." So awful did its disgusting, stringy meat taste that the Dutch called it "loathsome bird." Huge and flightless, it could be 1m (3ft) tall, had a massive, hooked beak, and looked like an oddball. It lived on the island of Mauritius and became extinct in the 17th century. Humans cruelly hunted the dodo as its lack of flight made it easy prey.

SUPER EAGLE

Haast's eagles, larger than the largest vultures, flew at a super-fast 80kph (50mph), swooping down on prey as big as the flightless moa, 15 times the weight of an eagle. Striking with huge talons, they would rip their victims apart with their beaks, causing death by blood loss. Inhabitants of New Zealand, Haast's eagles became extinct in about 1500, when humans hunted the moa to extinction.

Australia 24c
Thylacine (Tasmanian Tiger)
Endangered Species

TIGER WOLF

The Tasmanian tiger was a bizarre cross between a tiger and a wolf, could both growl and hiss, and carried its young in a pouch like a kangaroo. The size of a large dog, it had a striped back and ruthlessly hunted down kangaroos, wallabies, and wombats in its native Australia. Although extinct on the Australian mainland for centuries, it survived on the island of Tasmania until the early 20th century.

HALF ZEBRA

The totally weird quagga looked as if the front half of a zebra and the back half of a horse had been stitched together. Its face, neck, and chest were striped, while its back was plain brown. A close relative of the zebra, it lived in Africa. It was discovered in the late 18th century, but wiped out within 100 years by cunning human hunters who were after its meat and hide. The last quagga died in Amsterdam Zoo in 1883.

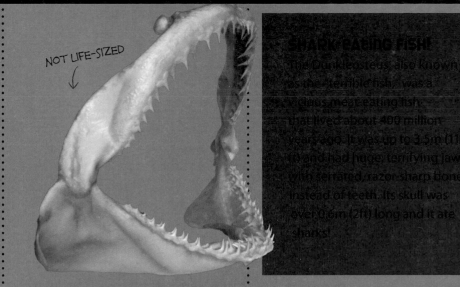

NOT LIFE-SIZED

SHARK-EATING FISH!

The Dunkleosteus, also known as the "terrible fish," was a ferocious meat-eating fish that lived about 400 million years ago. It was up to 3.5m (11.5 ft) and had huge, terrifying jaws, with serrated, razor-sharp bones instead of teeth. Its skull was over 0.6m (2ft) long and it ate sharks!

HAIRY ELEPHANT

Some species of mammoth really were totally mammoth. Much larger than their living relative, the elephant, they were at least 5m (16ft) tall, with lethal tusks measuring more than 3.4m (11ft). They used both tusks to attack their enemies. In 2007, the carcass of a one-month-old woolly mammoth was discovered in Russia, where it had been buried for an incredible 37,000 years.

FIERCE WARRIORS

The Celts enjoyed drinking alcohol, feasting, gambling, and, most of all, fighting. The warriors covered themselves with blue paint called woad and washed their hair in lime water to make it stand up in spikes. Even the Romans were scared of these mad-looking warriors, who would scream and shout while they attacked without fear.

CELTIC WEAPONS

The Celts, who originated in Central Europe almost 3,000 years ago, ran riot throughout Europe due to the fierceness of their weapons. They used slings to break the bones and fracture the skulls of their enemies from a distance, and would shower them with deadly spears. The Celts would then plunge into hand-to-hand battle with vicious curved, double-edged, pointed swords, slashing and stabbing in a wild frenzy. The few opponents who survived the onslaught were turned into slaves.

BURNING THE DEAD

The early Celts would cover the dead with the skins of sheep and cows, bind the body, and bury it with anything else they thought the dead person would need in the afterlife. For important people, slaves, animals such as horses and dogs, portions of meat, weapons, clothing, and tools. They believed that the dead would go to another world and would need all these things.

THE LAST CELTS

The Romans conquered most of the Celts in Europe, slaughtering hundreds of thousands of their warriors. Most of the remaining Celts got used to the Roman way of life, but parts of Britain and Ireland remained Celtic strongholds. They kept on savagely attacking and killing any Romans who came near them, so the Romans eventually gave up.

SLAVE TRADE

The Romans hated the Celts. They thought they were uncivilized barbarians. However, they traded the high-quality clothing and glassware that the Celts made, as well as the slaves they captured. In exchange, the Celts were given wine, which they loved but did not know how to make. The Celts would give the Romans a slave for just one jar of wine.

HUMAN VICTIMS

The religious leaders of the Celts were called Druids. They were the teachers, priests, doctors, lawmakers, and judges. Druidism was one of the few religions that the Romans tried to wipe out because it involved human sacrifices. When they wanted to find out about something very important, Druids would plunge a knife into the chest of a human. They thought that the sacrifice would help them predict the future.

SMELLY FAMILIES

All members of a Celtic family used to live and sleep together in one big room, sometimes with their animals, so it would be a very smelly home. They had knives for cutting up food, but they did not have forks and most people did not own a spoon. They used to eat with their fingers. The Roman Julius Caesar thought it was odd that the Celts believed that it was unlawful to eat hares and geese: they raised them as pets instead.

WOMEN FIGHTERS

Most Celtic men were warriors, but so were some women, including the famous Queen Boudicca. She had a chariot with sharp spikes sticking out from the wheels so she could mow the enemy down as she charged into them. The British queen hated the Romans and burnt down the towns of London and Colchester in AD60. She was eventually defeated and died by poisoning.

ICE-PICK IN THE BRAIN

Dr. Walter Freeman (1895–1972) had a cavalier attitude to brain surgery. He performed an astonishing 3,500 lobotomies during his career – an operation to cut the nerves between two parts of the brain – at first using an ice-pick taken from his kitchen at home. He didn't work in a hospital theater, preferring to travel round the U.S.A. performing the ops in his "lobotomobile." Once, he invited some journalists to watch him work, and to their horror his ice-pick slipped into the patient's brain and killed him. Unmoved, Freeman started work on the next person in line.

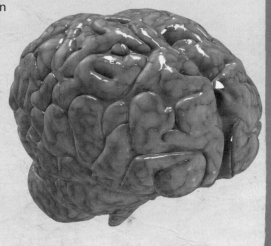

GOATY CURES

During the 1920s and 30s, U.S. conman and doctor John R. Brinkley promised to cure people of over 25 ailments including lung disease, high blood pressure, insanity, and even wind, by implanting them with goat glands! His exaggerated health claims had people flocking to his clinic for treatment, which he sometimes performed when drunk. He was sued many times for killing people with his wacky cures.

GLADIATORS' SECRETS

Galen, one of the most influential physicians during Roman times, knew more than anyone else about anatomy, surgery, and the way the human body works. He got his knowledge first-hand while treating the appalling wounds received by Roman gladiators – stabbings, severed limbs, smashed bones, gruesome head injuries, and flesh torn by wild animals.

BIRD BEAKS

Doctors in the Middle Ages didn't want to get too close to their plague-ridden patients, so they'd visit victims wearing leather breeches, a head-to-foot overcoat, a wide-brimmed hat, and a weird bird-beak mask filled with aromatic herbs, which made them look like gruesome giant crows. They'd also prod people from afar with long wooden canes.

GLORIOUS MUD

Like many 18th-century medical students, James Graham never finished his studies, but he still became one of the most famous and popular doctors in Britain. He gave his patients many gruesome and pointless treatments including electro-magnetic shocks and "earthbathing," which involved taking very long mud baths. He was so keen on the benefits of wallowing in mud that he gave public lectures while buried up to his neck in the stuff.

SLASH AND BURN

The Greek surgeon Archagathus was known as the Butcher. His favorite method of treatment was to chop the affected bit off, then "cauterize" the wound – basically burn it shut with a red-hot iron pulled from the fire.

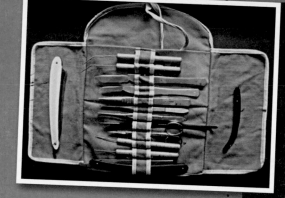

DEAD OR ALIVE?

Italian scientist Giovanni Aldini used to travel round Europe making newly dead bodies move – by stimulating their muscles with electric currents so their faces twitched, teeth chattered, eyes rolled, jaws opened, and arms and legs quivered. Many spectators were sure he was making the dead come back to life.

SPURIOUS SAWBONES

Ferdinand Waldo Demara Jr. was a great imposter who spent his life pretending to be other people. During the Korean War he masqueraded as a surgeon, joined the Royal Canadian Navy, and had to carry out various life and death operations on 16 severely wounded men. It's said that he had a photographic memory and grabbed a textbook beforehand to memorize the procedures, but it's still amazing that none of the men died.

PHANTOM FACES

During December 1924, the huge, eerie faces of 2 dead sailors were seen floating in the waters alongside the oil tanker SS *Watertown*. These disembodied apparitions appeared night after night at dusk as the ship sailed towards the Panama Canal – and during its next 2 voyages, too. Most of the sailors say they saw the phantom faces, and the captain even took a photograph of them! The 2 men had died in a freak accident and their bodies were thrown overboard. Some say they returned to haunt the survivors because they were unhappy about their method of burial.

FLYING DUTCHMAN

The *Flying Dutchman* must be the spookiest ghost ship of all. To see it floating with its eerie lights ablaze is considered an omen of doom and disaster. The story goes that the sailors on board fell ill with the bubonic plague. The diseased ship was turned away from port after port until water and food ran out and the whole crew died, their souls doomed to wander the high seas for eternity. Those who've seen the ship say the decks are littered with corpses, with a smiling dead man beckoning over the side, his back being pecked by a seagull.

SEE-THROUGH SOLDIERS

At the muddy battlefield of Mons, Belgium, in World War I, newspapers reported that a huge spectral army was seen floating in the sky above the trenches. Some said it was the army of St. George and his sword-carrying warriors urging on the British troops, who were vastly outnumbered by the Germans.

BURNING BOAT

In 1752, off the Rhode Island coast of the U.S.A., wreckers burnt a Dutch boat – not realizing that a woman remained on board. People still claim to see a burning boat off the New England shore, with a woman in white on the decks screaming for her life.

FOREVER FIGHTING

Ghostly soldiers are often said to be seen re-fighting the Battle of Little Bighorn in Montana, U.S.A. In 1876, Sitting Bull's Cheyenne and Lakota Native Americans massacred U.S. General Custer and his 7th Cavalry. People regularly report hearing frightening screams of grisly deaths and seeing spectral fights between the combatants. General Custer's ghost is occasionally seen at the Battlefield Museum while ghostly Cheyenne warriors on horses are seen riding around the battle site.

BATTLE ECHOES

Two Englishwomen on holiday near the town of Dieppe in France were woken up early one morning in 1951 by the sounds of gunfire shots and dive-bombing planes. They listened for the next 3 hours to the echoing screams and shots of a battle being re-enacted. Nine years earlier, during World War II, the British had attacked Dieppe and been massacred, and the women's accounts of the ghostly sounds of fighting bore an uncanny resemblance to the actual battle events of that day.

LIFESAVING SPECTER!

A British officer called William Speight says he saw a phantom figure in his trench dugout one night during World War I. The specter apparently pointed to an area on the ground, then floated away. Worried, Speight ordered the area to be excavated next day – and found a narrow tunnel packed with mines which were primed to explode in 13 hours' time. The ghostly specter had saved the soldiers' lives!

SPIRITS OF THE DROWNED

The *Caleuche* is a ghost ship which haunts the seas off the island of Chiloé, Chile. People who see it say it's always brightly lit, with the tinkling of party music and people laughing. Spookily, the ship is said to contain the spirits of all those drowned at sea, collected up by mermaids. The *Caleuche* only appears for a minute or so every night, before disappearing under the seas.

HEAD OF THE FAMILY

In 1536, when Henry VIII arranged the death of his wife, Anne Boleyn, an expert swordsman was brought over from France. Henry wanted her to die swiftly and thought English executioners would make a mess of the job.

CHOP, CHOP

The guillotine was a tall upright frame on which a sharp, angled blade was suspended by a rope. A prisoner would kneel at the base of the frame, with their neck sticking out. When the rope was released, the blade would hurtle down at great speed, decapitating the prisoner. Sometimes, a basket would be placed on the floor, ready to catch the head. The guillotine became the favorite method of execution during the French Revolution.

UGH!
THE FRENCH GUILLOTINE BECAME KNOWN AS "THE NATIONAL RAZOR."

FIRST GUILLOTINE EXECUTION

The first victim of the guillotine was Nicolas Jacques Pelletier on 25 April 1792. He was a highwayman who had been caught after robbing a man in Paris, France. He was sentenced to death but had to wait 3 months while the guillotine was built and tested on corpses taken from a hospital. The guillotine was painted red and Pelletier also wore a red shirt for the occasion. The guillotine severed his head straightaway.

MAXIMILIEN ROBESPIERRE

The early years after the French Revolution were known as the Reign of Terror, which was masterminded by Maximilien Robespierre. Up to 40,000 people were sentenced to death by execution. Not only nobles were executed, but also politicians, philosophers, prostitutes, and common criminals. The reasons for execution became so meaningless that the people turned against Robespierre. He shared the same fate as his victims: he was executed by guillotine in 1794.

DEAD HEAD

One gruesome guillotining happened in France in 1905. Henri Languille's severed head somehow landed back on his neck after the chop. A doctor, waiting for the twitching to end, called out Languille's name and was astonished when the dead man's eyes moved and focused on his own. The doctor called his name again, and the same thing happened. He did it again, but this time, there was no response. It had taken 25 to 30 seconds for the head to be dead.

THE KING'S HEAD

An early victim of the guillotine was the French King Louis XVI, who was beheaded in 1793. The French people had revolted against the monarchy and deposed the king in 1792. King Louis had a messy death. Unusually, the blade did not cut straight through his neck first time, so it had to be lowered again. The crowd surged forward and dipped their handkerchiefs in his blood.

UNHAPPY CROWDS

A huge crowd watched the first use of the guillotine in Paris, but they were unhappy with its speed. They were used to watching much slower executions by hanging or by the Catherine wheel, which they found horrific but entertaining. They shouted out that they wanted to bring back the gallows, but the guillotine started to gain huge support and crowds flocked to the beheadings.

TOWER OF DEATH

In the 16th century, the Tower of London in England became the most famous place in the world for executions. Most of the victims were beheaded, including the Countess of Salisbury, who survived 10 decapitation attempts with an axe before she finally died. After an execution, the victim's severed head was held up by the hair so the huge crowd could see the dead person's face.

TO DIE FOR

Cosmetics can be deadly. Women used to powder their faces with white powder containing lead, then rouge their cheeks with vermilion, which contained mercury. These poisons caused skin eruptions and scarring, so even more toxic powder was put on top to cover the blemishes. One of the first martyrs to beauty was Maria Gunning, who married the Earl of Coventry. A famous beauty, she died in 1760 at the age of 27 from blood poisoning caused by painting her face with white lead.

WIDE-EYED BEAUTIES

Italian ladies used to put a tincture of belladonna – which means "beautiful woman" – into their eyes. Belladonna is an extract of the deadly nightshade plant, and the poison would enlarge the pupil, making the eye appear bigger and more attractive. But it also blurred the women's vision and after a while caused blindness.

MODERN HAZARD

Nail polish is classified as hazardous waste by some local regulatory bodies around the world because it often contains formaldehyde – used to embalm dead bodies – and other toxic substances. Nail polish remover is gruesome, too. It contains acetone and benzene, chemicals which can damage the nervous system and cause sickness, drowsiness, and injure the lungs, liver, and kidneys.

WEE IS EVERYWHERE

Many face creams, hair conditioners, lotions, and cleansers contain urea, which is found in wee. Urea is a waste product made by humans and mammals – the average person creates about 30g (1oz) a day. But it can also be made by heating ammonia and carbon dioxide at very high temperatures. In some urea-containing face creams, you can still smell the sharp, acrid aroma of wee.

FAKE NAILS

Artificial fingernails can be breeding grounds and transport vehicles for bacteria. In 1997, a woman died in a Californian hospital after surgery. The deadly bacteria was traced back to the artificial fingernails of a nurse who was tending her.

WHAT'S UNDER THAT LABEL?

Some anti-ageing creams are made from the tissue of pregnant women or animals. There are anti-wrinkle creams which boast that they contain placenta, the nutrient-rich, liver-like organ which develops during pregnancy to feed the baby.

BLACK EYES

The kohl eyeliner that Egyptian, Roman, and Middle Eastern women used to wear was made from antimony. In small doses, antimony causes headaches, dizziness, and depression, and in large doses it's a poison that acts in a very similar way to arsenic.

NIGHTINGALE DROPPINGS

For centuries, Japanese Geisha entertainers and Kabuki actors painted their faces with thick white stage make-up – then cleaned it off with powdered nightingale droppings. There are nightingale farms in Japan where the poo is collected, then heat-treated to make sure it is free of bacteria. Nowadays, expensive creams and lotions made of nightingale droppings are popular with celebrities in the West, too.

BUG COLONY

Mascara is the most gruesomely germy of all cosmetics. The wands provide a moist, dark breeding ground for germs called Pseudomonas to thrive. The older the mascara wand, the more bacteria it will contain – and if the wearer ever licks or wets the wand, lots more bacteria will jump in there too. It's dangerous when someone pokes or scratches the surface of their eye while applying mascara. They can get a nasty eye infection or even an ulcer on the surface of the eye from the bacteria which instantly infect the wound.

UGH!
IN THE MIDDLE AGES, WOMEN DYED BLACK HAIR BROWN USING OIL OF VITRIOL, A HIGHLY TOXIC SULFURIC ACID!

CHILI WORMS

Mopane worms are wriggly, hair-covered caterpillars which make a juicy meal. Their guts are squeezed out first, and then they are fried with onions and tomatoes, with a touch of chili sauce to give the grubby dish an extra kick. In parts of Africa, mopane worms are so popular that they are becoming scarce.

STINKING FISH HEADS

Fish smells truly awful when it goes off, but some people actually like to eat it when it is rotten. Called stinkheads, rotting fish are a favorite food of the Yupik Eskimos of Alaska. The head and guts of whitefish such as salmon are mixed together in a barrel, covered with burlap, and buried in the ground for a week so that they go rotten and ferment. You might need to hold your nose when you eat this.

FRUIT BAT SOUP

Fruit bats are hairy flying rodents, but in Palau in Micronesia they are also the main ingredient in a tasty traditional soup. Whole bats are put in boiling water with onions, salt, and ginger to make a broth. The bats are then taken out and skinned. Their meat is then returned to the broth, which is finished off with some more chopped onions and soy sauce.

MAGGOT AND SOY

Hundreds of wriggling bee larvae are used to make hachinoko, a nauseating dish found in some areas of Japan. The yellow bee maggots are cooked in soy sauce and sugar. The result has a sweet, crumbly texture. Hachinoko became popular as a source of protein while there was a scarcity of meat and fish, but it is now rarely eaten.

StUFFeD MICe

The Ancient Romans loved to eat stuffed dormice, and the little rodents are still eaten today in some parts of the world. Called "glires," the Roman recipe involved skinning the mouse, removing its intestines, and stuffing it with a mixture of pork, bits of mouse, pepper, and nuts. The mouse would be put in a casserole dish and baked in the oven.

JeLLieD MOOSe NOSe

The revolting, mucus-filled nose of a moose is turned into a wobbly delicacy in the famous Canadian jellied moose nose dish. The moose's nose is carefully cleaned of all mucus and hairs, and it is boiled with onion, spices, garlic, and vinegar. The bones are then taken out of the nose and the meat is left in its broth to jellify. It is then sliced and eaten cold.

OFFAL TAStY

Cockscombs are the red, blue, or gray fleshy crests on the heads of turkeys, chickens, and other domestic fowl. The French, who eat most things, call them "crêtes de coq" and often slit them, stuff them, and fry them. Cockscombs are said to have a wobbly, jelly-like texture and to taste rather similar to frog's legs. Almost as bad as eating them is preparing them. The feathers have to be plucked out, the cockscombs are soaked in lemon juice to soften the thick outer skin, which is then carefully peeled off so as not to lose the shape of the tips.

Sea COCKROACH StiR-FRY

Mole crabs are just like marine cockroaches, with ugly insect bodies and creepy-crawly legs. Looking at a bowl of them wriggling around is enough to make some people sick, but in Southeast Asia, people love eating them in a stir-fry or deep-fried whole in tempura batter as a crunchy, bite-sized snack.

POINT THAT FINGER!

Lee Redmond didn't cut her fingernails for 30 years, and by the end of it they measured a combined length of 8.65m (28ft 4in) – her right thumbnail alone was 90cm (2ft 11in) long. She says her long nails didn't cause her any discomfort in daily life. She could wash-up, drive, ride a bike – the only thing she found difficult was pulling on a thick, heavy coat.

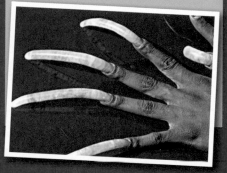

TOENAIL QUEEN

In the 1990s, American Louise Hollis grew her toenails over 15cm (6in) long – all 10 toenails together reached a length of 2.21m (87in). She always had to wear open-toed shoes so it's lucky she lived somewhere warm like California!

MUSTACHE MAGIC

Some men grow their mustaches and beards so long they can make living sculptures out of them. Elmar Weisser of the Swabian Beard Club in Germany has created the Tower of London and a "Beard Castle" from his facial hair, while at the 2009 World Beard and Mustache Championships in Alaska, Dave Traver wove his into the shape of a snowshoe.

FELINE FEAT

Following an ancient Native American Indian tradition, Huron Indian Dennis Avner has transformed himself into a "human tiger." An Indian wise man chose the tiger as his special animal spirit guide. Mr. Avner now calls himself "Stalking Cat," eats raw meat, and climbs trees. He wears green contact lenses with slit pupils, has pointy, cat-shaped teeth, and has undergone various operations to make his face appear more cat-like. He even wears whiskers!

WHAT A STRETCH!

Garry Turner from England has a rare medical condition that means his skin is extra-stretchy. He once pulled the skin on his stomach 15.8cm (6.25in) away from his body, and he can perform a very unusual trick called the human turtleneck, in which he pulls his neck skin upward to cover his mouth! This incredible elasticity is due to Ehlers-Danlos Syndrome, a disorder which affects the tissue connecting the skin to the body.

BLOOD ARt

Artist Marc Quinn once made a frozen sculpture of his head out of his own blood. He made a silicone cast of his head, filled it with 9 pints of blood – taken over a 5-month period – then put it in a refrigerated perspex box for show at art galleries. The head has toured the world, and in 2005 was sold to a U.S. art collector for $2.16m (£1.5m).

BiG FOOt

The tallest man ever recorded was American Robert Pershing Wadlow, who died in 1940. He was 2.72m (8ft 11in) tall, which is about 36cm taller than the current tallest living man. Mr. Wadlow had whopping 47cm (1ft 6in) feet and his hands measured 32.3cm (12¾in) from his wrist to his longest finger. To keep his weight over the 200kg (31st) mark, he used to eat about 8,000 calories a day, 3 times the recommended daily allowance for men.

MONSTER BEARDS

Shamsher Singh from India started growing his beard years ago. It was last measured at 1.83m (6ft) long, which must get in his way when he's doing the vacuuming. But Mr. Singh's achievement is dwarfed by that of Hans Langreth from Norway. When he died in 1927, his beard had reached an astonishing 5.33m (17ft 6in). He used to keep it rolled in a pouch under his neck, to stop people pulling on it and asking if it was real.

EGG FAKER

The killer cuckoo chick is probably the most violent youngster in the animal kingdom, born to one of the worst parents. The mother is too lazy to raise her young, so lays her egg in the nest of the reed warbler, who unknowingly treats it as one of her own. The cuckoo hatches before the reed warbler's chicks, grows to be a monster many times their size, then kills them so that it can have all the food for itself.

RODENT RELATIONS

Rats and mice sometimes eat their own young when things get overcrowded in the litter. A mother rat kept as a pet may even eat her children if she is hungry or stressed. She tends to eat the wounded or deformed infants first. Female rats also kill the young of another female in order to take control of the nest.

COLD FEET

Male emperor penguins have a very tough parenting job as their female partners go on vacation to find food, leaving them to look after their egg in horrendous, ice-cold weather conditions. For 65 days, the father stands with the egg balanced on his toes, as it will freeze if it touches the ice. He has to endure temperatures of -70°C (-94°F) and winds of 160kph (100mph) before the mother finally returns.

BAD DRAGON

The giant, brutal Komodo dragon, which looks like a leftover from the age of the dinosaurs, is too lazy to look after its young and will sometimes gorge a baby up as a snack. The monster lizards, which can be 3m (10ft) long, cannot be bothered to build their own nests, so lay their eggs in the abandoned nesting mounds of scrubfowl. When the eggs hatch, the babies have to scramble up the nearest tree for protection from their own cannibalistic relatives.

TERRIBLE FATHER

The male seahorse may act like nature's best dad, carefully carrying the eggs in its own pouch, but it is one of the worst. The dad does absolutely nothing for the babies as soon as they are born. Most of them are carried away by currents or eaten by predators. Only 5 out of every 1,000 infants survive.

BAD MOM!

Scorpions are not good mothers. If one of their babies climbs off their backs to go wandering, they will eat it. They will also eat sickly infants. Sometimes the mother gets very disturbed or stressed by something that's going on around, so will wolf down a few of her young to calm her nerves.

VICIOUS MONKEY DADS

Some animals are known for eating their young. In the animal communities of the hanuman langur, India's sacred monkey, family struggles are particularly vicious. The strongest male monkeys compete for control of the group, and the one who eventually wins will try to bite to death the offspring of the previous chief of the group.

WHERE'S MOM?

Female octopuses find pregnancy very difficult. They cannot hunt while they are looking after their eggs and sometimes have to ingest their own arms for food. By the time the eggs hatch, the octopus is too weak to look after its young or defend itself, so it is usually eaten by predators. The young are left to fend for themselves, and are often gobbled up.

SLAVE KILLERS

Trainee Spartan soldiers, in around 11BC, had to kill a slave as part of their military training. Before becoming a full member of the Spartan army, the trainee was made to ambush and murder a "helot," which was a type of slave who worked as a laborer for the Spartan state. To make them tough, Spartan soldiers were made to eat pork boiled in blood.

THE TOUGH SPARTANS

Life was very hard for Spartan boys. All children were owned by the state, rather than by their parents. Healthy boys were sent to boarding school where they learnt to endure incredible pain and hardship. They were forced to sleep outside in the rain and cold, and were not allowed to wear shoes. Every day involved tough military training. As soon as they left school, they all had to join the Spartan army. They were not allowed to surrender and had to fight to the death.

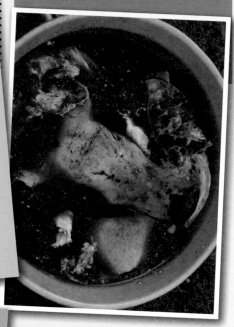

WOW!
ONLY HALF THE CHILDREN BORN TO ANCIENT GREEK FAMILIES LIVED TO THE AGE OF 18.

CUTTING UP BODIES

A Greek called Herophilus was the first person to cut up dead bodies to see how they were put together. He took them apart to see how the muscles, bones, and organs worked. He was then able to tell doctors how they should treat their patients' injuries.

GREEK FIGHTING

In battle, foot soldiers formed squares of 256 soldiers, called a phalanx. The first five rows of soldiers would hold very long, sharp spears (up to 6m/18ft long) in front of them, so that they could kill their enemy without having to get too close to them.

WAR HELMET

READY FOR WAR

At 14, most Greek boys were sent to wrestling school where they learned to fight and were trained in athletics, javelin-throwing, and discus-hurling. They did not learn these skills for fun, though. They were being taught the skills of war. After wrestling school, they spent another 2 years completing their military training.

SENT INTO EXILE

The Greeks of Athens were the first people to govern themselves rather than being ruled by a king, but they were not very tolerant of their fellow citizens. Once a year the citizens would decide who they did not like: the person with the greatest number of votes would be made to leave the city for 10 years.

THE GREEK GODS

The Ancient Greeks believed in many gods, whom they thought would kill them, make them ill, or ruin their lives if they were angry. The Greeks presented the gods with gifts to make sure that nothing bad happened to them. If they wanted a special favor, they would kill animals as a sacrifice to the gods, spilling their blood all over an altar.

THE DEADLY SIEGE

Ancient Greece was split into different city-states which were often at war with one another, and also fought neighboring kingdoms. The Spartans ganged up with the Persians to defeat the state of Athens. Instead of trying to defeat the Athenian army, they cut off all food supplies to the city. Thousands of Athenians starved to death, so eventually the city had to surrender.

MiGHtY MOUSe

Scientists have created a gruesome, genetically modified super-mouse which is much more aggressive and 10 times more active than normal mice. It can run for 5 hours without getting tired, eat twice as much without getting fat, and lives much longer than normal mice. Now they're seeing if they can do the same for humans!

SUPER MOUSE!

AiR SHOW DiSASteR

At the Paris Air show in 1973, the Russians unveiled the supersonic Tupolev TU-144 aircraft, their answer to the British-French Concorde. But on its display flight doing maneuvers, the plane hit trouble. With thousands of people watching, it suddenly stalled and plunged into a steep dive, then broke into pieces in the air. The accident was thought to be caused by a failure of the high-tech autostabilization input controls, which balance the plane under high stresses and pressure.

TitAniC SinkS

The most forward-thinking technology of the time was used to build the luxury liner the *Titanic*, and everyone believed it was unsinkable. But on its first voyage an iceberg hit its hull and the ship broke up and sank – it now rests at the bottom of the Atlantic. More than 1,500 people died, only 705 surviving the catastrophe. Over 300 bodies were found floating in the sea the next morning. They all had life jackets on so could have been saved, but they died of hypothermia, which occurs when the body gets below 35ºC (95ºF), and exhaustion, from being immersed in the icy cold waters.

EXPLODiNG PHOneS

Cellphones have been known to kill people. One man changed his phone's battery and put it in his breast pocket, when it blew up. One of the fragments severed the major artery in his neck and he bled to death. Another man's cellphone exploded while he was working in an iron mill, and he died from chest wounds – the intense heat in the mill caused the inflammable liquid inside the battery to blow.

HINDENBURG HORROR

The Hindenburg was the largest-ever zeppelin, a grand and luxurious German airship which carried passengers across the Atlantic. It was docking in New Jersey on a trip from Europe when disaster hit. People saw a small mushroom-shaped flame at the rear of the airship, there was a muffled explosion and suddenly the tail end became a blow torch shooting huge flames into the sky. Inside, people were being crashed around the state rooms and cabins, and lucky ones jumped out of the windows as their only chance of survival. In less than a minute, the whole airship was ablaze and plunged tail-first to crash on the ground. 35 of the 93 people on board died.

MIRACLE MAN

When he went to retrieve his cellphone from the rail-track where he'd dropped it, Noah Hodgkiss got hit by a high-speed train thundering past. He was knocked several meters into the air, but survived his technology-inspired terror.

BLOW UP LAPTOPS

In 2004, computers started spontaneously combusting on people's desks. One computer burst into flames at a conference in Japan, and a video of the smoldering, melting laptop was quickly sent round the world. In India, a man was found charred and dead on top of his burned-out computer. Other laptops started belching out black smoke and massively overheating. When the problem was investigated, it was found that the lithium ion batteries were overheating and causing the laptops to burst into flames.

OWL EMISSIONS

Owls are great regurgitators, spitting out small, hairy, sausage-shaped pellets a couple of times a day. These contain mashed-up bones, teeth, claws, beaks, fur, and feathers that the owl can't digest. When owls catch a mouse, bird or fish, they swallow it whole. It passes through the first stomach or gizzard, where it gets ground up a bit, before going into the owl's proper stomach. There, the tough bony bits get squeezed back into the gizzard, then coughed up 6–8 hours later as an owl pellet. Amazingly, quite unlike human sick, owl pellets don't smell bad at all.

DEATH BY HAIRBALL

Cats keep their fur very neat and tidy by licking it, but all that grooming can cause problems. Their tongues are like sandpaper and catch lots of hair, which the cat then swallows. Sometimes they swallow so much hair that it forms into balls inside their stomachs. Then they spend a lot of time trying to cough or sick these up. Cows and rabbits also get hairballs, but because these animals cannot vomit, they're usually discovered only after their death.

MAGICAL HAIRBALLS

Lumps of undigested foreign matter such as hair, bones, and food have been found in the stomachs and intestines of animals for centuries. These are called bezoars (say it "bee-zures") and were very popular in the Middle Ages as people thought they had magical and medicinal powers. Doctors used them to "cure" epilepsy, dysentery, the plague, and as an antidote to poison and snake bites.

HAIRY CYSTS

Lots of different types of cysts can form in the body, but one of the most gruesome has its own hair, nails, bone, and even teeth! When you cut it open, you see long bits of hair and little teeth wrapped in it. It's called a dermoid cyst, and can grow quite large – up to about 15cm (6in) across.

RAPUNZEL SYNDROME

Some people like to chew their own hair and occasionally they swallow it. This long stringy hairball, called a trichobezoar (say it "trick-o-bee-zure"), can get stuck in their stomach. Some of the twisted hair strands can also move into the intestines, so the hairball is stretched out lengthways between the stomach and gut. This is called Rapunzel syndrome, after the fairy-tale princess with very long hair.

JUST GOOD FRIENDS

In 1897, a big hairball was removed from a chicken. The pet chicken was apparently good friends with a dog and used to peck and groom it, often swallowing the dog's hair. As a result, a hairball had grown so large inside the chicken's craw (its "first" stomach) that it couldn't take in any more food and was starving to death. The chicken hairball was surgically removed and is now on display in the National Museum of Health and Medicine in Washington D.C.

WHAT A WHOPPER!

Cysts are sacs that can grow in the body, and some reach huge proportions. When doctors removed a cyst from inside 18-year-old Sarah Borthwick, they said it was as big as a "dinosaur egg." It weighed 6kg (13lb) and the doctor needed both hands to hold it.

HARD TACK

On long voyages, sailors used to eat "hard tack" or "pilot bread," a basic biscuit made of flour, salt, and water. The biscuits were stored so long on board that by the time they came to be eaten, they were usually riddled with weevils and other nasty insects. On Captain Cook's 1769 voyage, one sailor wrote that he could shake thousands of "vermin" off a single hard tack biscuit. He said the weevils tasted hot and strong like mustard mixed with ammonia.

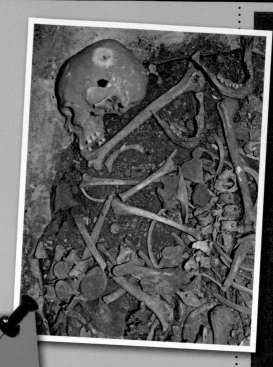

MOCK TURTLE SOUP

In 18th- and 19th-century Europe, green turtle soup was considered a huge delicacy, but it was very expensive because the turtles had to be shipped from the West Indies. So people used calves' heads instead of turtles and called it mock turtle soup. They boiled the calves' heads in water, adding oysters or fish to mimic the rich turtle flavor.

← YUK!!

PRAIRIE OYSTER

This drink is made of an unbeaten raw egg with the yolk still whole – which looks like an oyster – gently swizzled with some Worcestershire sauce, then drunk down in one big gulp. People drink it in the mornings to perk themselves up after a heavy night.

BABY'S HEAD

In England, a suet pudding is traditionally known as a "baby's head." People used to eat baby's head with gravy as the main course, followed by baby's head with custard for pudding!

PUPPY PIE

Every year in Painswick, England, people make puppy pies – luckily without any puppies in them. They're meat or fruit pies cooked with a little china dog inside and on top. The tradition arose long ago when locals were accused of serving dog pies to their visitors. The locals got so angry they started making mock puppy pies instead. The meat versions are often served with bow-wow sauce, a pungent mix of vinegar, mustard, and pickled walnuts.

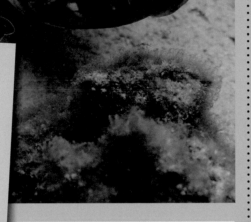

BOMBAY DUCK

Don't be taken in if you see this on a restaurant menu: it's not duck at all but a slender, slimy lizardfish about 15 to 20cm (6 to 8in) long. It's usually salted and sun-dried, a process which makes it so stinky it has to be transported in special airtight containers. Some people think Bombay duck's pongy flavor and super-salty, gruesomely gritty texture are delicious and eat it deep-fried as a starter or in curries. It's also known as "bummalo."

MAGGOTY MEAT

Rich men's cooks in the Middle Ages liked making jokes with their food creations, and one of the favorites was "maggoty meat." This was fried meat served while it was still sizzling, scattered at the last minute with tiny slivers of raw heart which would wriggle about in the heat like living maggots.

WHITE PUDDING

It may be white, but it's not a pudding as most people know it. In fact, it's a sausage filled with large amounts of stodgy lard, suet, or other white fat, with a bit of oatmeal added to bulk it out. If that wasn't enough lardy content, in Scotland they often deep-fry it, too, so it's crispy on the outside and soggy inside.

POO BOMB

In the 11th century, armies used to chuck human poo bombs at each other – a recipe has survived from 1044! This noxious concoction included whopping amounts of dried, powdered, human excrement mixed with the poisons wolfsbane, aconite, and arsenic, plus dried bean pods to create wafts of toxic black smoke.

GOOD FOR THE GARDEN?

Poo and wee are often used as fertilizers. Human waste contains chemicals including nitrogen, phosphorus, potassium, and calcium in higher quantities than are found in most garden fertilizers. This makes them a cheap and green way to enrich the land. Sometimes people put their wastes straight on to the ground, when it is called "night soil." But this can be unhealthy. Most human waste is composted or processed first. "Humanure" is composed of wee, poo, the paper used to dispose of it, and sawdust. It is left to compost naturally at high temperatures for a year or 2 before being put on the land.

TANNING HIDES

To turn animal skins into supple leather, both feces and urine were used in olden times. The skins were cleaned then soaked in urine to remove hairs. Next they were pounded for several hours with dung – most often dog, human, or bird poo – to soften them. Often the tanners would employ children called dung gatherers. They were sent out to scavenge excrement and collect human wee from the urine pots on street corners for use in the tanning process.

WEE BATTERY

In Singapore, scientists have come up with a brilliant, cheap, and gruesome idea – a tiny battery that's powered by wee. It's for use in home health tests. The chemicals in a person's urine give clues about diseases, such as diabetes, that they might be suffering from. By using wee to power this ingenious battery, 1.5v of electricity is generated – enough to analyze the wee that's making it work!

PITCH SOME POOP

Cowpats are more useful than you think. They can be burnt as fuel and are also the main ingredient in dung-throwing contests. In Beaver, Oklahoma, there's an annual cow-chip chucking contest, where dried cow pats over 15cm (6in) wide are thrown frisbee-style across a field. The record throw is an astonishing 56m (185ft), recorded in 2001.

CHEW ON THAT!

The chemical compound urea, which can be extracted from urine, is sometimes used in the manufacture of baked goods such as pretzels to give them their lovely deep brown color.

HOLY COW!

In India, where the cow is considered a sacred animal, a special new drink made out of cow's wee is being created. It's called "gau jal" and it's a soft drink flavored with herbs that's meant to be a healthy substitute to cola. The bovine brew is likely to become popular: in parts of rural India, cow dung and urine are sometimes taken as part of religious purifying rituals.

URINE THERAPY

Some people like to massage their wee into their skin to soften it, while others swear by it as a health potion. It is called urine therapy. Morarji Desai, Prime Minister of India from 1977–79, was a keen urine drinker. Inspired by stories of its success, British actress Sarah Miles has been drinking her urine on a daily basis for over 30 years. She says it is a tonic and keeps allergies at bay. Doctors are less enthusiastic about the practice, and don't believe it provides any health benefits.

BAD LUCK BOOK

Can books be cursed? A London bookbinder called Francis Sangorski created one of the world's most ornate books – an illustrated edition of the *Rubaiyat of Omar Khayyam*. It was covered in silver, satinwood, ivory, and leather and inlaid with 1,050 jewels. But things went wrong immediately: nobody would buy the book, it eventually sold for less than half its worth, and was shipped to the U.S.A. – unfortunately on the *Titanic*. Six weeks later, Sangorski himself drowned. And when another binder recreated the book, it was bombed to smithereens in the London Blitz during WW II.

A HEX ON YOU!

Witches used to "hex" or put curses on people they didn't like, to make the milk of their cows run dry or their cattle go lame. In Ireland, people laid curses using eggs: by burying an egg on someone's land, you're thought to have "stolen" their luck. They also used special hex stones, which you turned three times while saying the name of the person you wanted to curse.

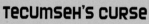

TECUMSEH'S CURSE

Tecumseh was the leader of the Shawnee tribe who was defeated in battle by the U.S. troops of William Henry Harrison. In 1840, Harrison became U.S. president and died a year into office. Since then, every U.S. president elected in a year ending in zero has died, often violently, while still president – a list that includes Abraham Lincoln, Franklin D. Roosevelt, and John F. Kennedy. People call it the curse of Tecumseh, but it was apparently broken when Ronald Reagan (elected 1980) survived an assassination attempt.

OTZI'S REVENGE

Otzi the Iceman fell into a glacier 5,300 years ago, and was discovered in 1991. Scientists soon started to do tests on his well-preserved remains – and the deaths began. A pathologist who'd picked up the body with his bare hands died the next year, a mountaineer who'd guided the team to Otzi was killed in an avalanche, a journalist who'd filmed the body's removal had a brain tumor… By 2005, seven people closely involved with Otzi had met their deaths.

THE CURSED BLUE HOPE DIAMOND

DIAMOND CURSE

The fabulous blue Hope diamond is thought to have brought bad luck to many of its owners. The huge diamond was supposedly stolen from a Hindu temple, and the priests put a curse on anyone who bought it. Marie Antoinette and Louis XVI lost their heads, the Hope family went bankrupt, the last owner's son died in a car crash, aged 9, while her daughter committed suicide and her husband was declared insane. It's now in the National Museum of Natural History, in Washington D.C.

FORWARD THINKING

Nostradamus was a French doctor who in 1555 wrote a book of obscure prophecies (in verse!) predicting plagues, wars, droughts, earthquakes, invasions, and the end of the world. Most of his predictions were too vague to be matched to any real events but he did seem to hit the button with the Fire of London in 1666 when he wrote: "The blood of the just will be demanded of London, Burnt by the fire of the year 66."

EEK! THE CAR ACTOR JAMES DEAN DIED IN – A SILVER PORSCHE 550 SPYDER – WAS SAID TO BE CURSED.

THE HAND OF THE MUMMY

Is there such a thing as the "Curse of Tutankhamun?" Weeks after King Tut's tomb was opened by archeologist Howard Carter and his benefactor Lord Caernarvon, the latter was killed by an infected mosquito bite. It was rumored that an inscription on the pharaoh's tomb read: "Death shall come on swift wings to him who disturbs the peace of the King," prophesying doom. Six years later, 11 people involved with the excavation team were dead, though Howard Carter himself lived for another 16 years.

UGLIEST FISH

The ugliest fish in the world is probably the fangtooth which, as its name suggests, has large, ferocious, piercing fangs. Compared to its body size, the fangtooth has the largest teeth in the oceans. They are so long that it has 2 holes on either side of its brain to accommodate them when it shuts its mouth. At 16cm (6in) long, the fish is only a miniature beast, though, and does not attack humans.

FISH CLEANERS

Cleaner fish have a truly disgusting job. Tiny in size, they live off the dead skin and parasites of larger fish, sometimes even cleaning between their teeth. The larger fish allow them to remove the dead matter and do not eat them, even though they eat many other fish of a similar size. One fish, the saber-toothed blenny, mimics the actions of a cleaner fish, but cheekily eats the healthy skin and scales of the larger fish instead.

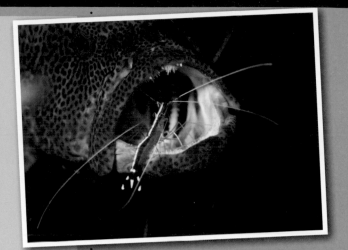

TONGUE-EATING LOUSE

The Cymothoa exigua, otherwise known as the tongue-eating louse, lives off the coast of California. It slowly eats the tongue of the spotted rose snapper fish. It then attaches itself to the tongue stub and pretends to be the fish's tongue, while feeding on its host's blood and mucus.

PIRANHA MYTH

Piranhas are often depicted as attacking humans in a mad frenzy and stripping all the flesh from their bones in just a few seconds. The vicious fish have very sharp teeth and a huge appetite for fresh meat. Piranhas do bite humans, sometimes out of sheer carelessness, but we are a bit too big for them to kill. They usually save their mass attacks for smaller animals.

WOW! THE ELECTRIC EEL CAN KILL A HUMAN WITH JUST ONE 500-VOLT SHOCK.

HUMAN KILLER

The biggest human killer in the seas is not the feared great white shark, but the innocent-looking jellyfish. They look like floating airbags, but their sting can be lethal. At least 50 people are killed by jellyfish each year. The deadliest are the box jellyfish and the Portuguese Man o' War. When they are touched, a lance pierces the victim's skin and poison flows through into the person, causing the body to go into shock.

THE LIVING DEAD

The lungfish is the zombie of the fish world. African and South American lungfish can play dead for up to 4 years. When the rivers dry out, they burrow into the mud and shut down their systems so that they seem to be almost dead. When the waters return, they come back to life again.

SEX CHANGE

Wrasse, which live in the oceans' coral reefs, can change sex. The largest adults, which claim a territory and dominate other wrasse, are always males. However, when the male dies, a female wrasse can change sex in just 6 or 7 days to become the male leader of the group.

FLESH SUCKER

The hagfish is a boneless, slime-covered tube with a peculiar, jaw-less mouth at one end. Its mouth is circular and lined with rows of teeth to help it suck on its prey, before tearing into its flesh. The hagfish's most gruesome feature is its habit of eating its way into its victim's body and then consuming all its flesh from the inside, leaving just the skin and bones.

DEATH BY SLEEPLESSNESS

This is claimed to be the worst disease anyone can get! Fatal familial insomnia is death due to not sleeping. First, people can't sleep for a couple of months, then they start sweating and hallucinating, become panicky, lose control of their bodies and can't speak. Eventually they fall into a coma and die. Luckily, this horrible disease is extremely rare and you can't catch it! It is caused by a genetic blip which makes big spongy holes in the sleep-producing area of the brain, called the thalamus.

AWFUL ANTHRAX

Anthrax is so deadly that it is used as a biological weapon. Inhaling the spores causes death in 75% of cases – people start off with a surprisingly mild flu but within a couple of days can barely breathe. They die from the lethal dose of toxins the bugs release into their bloodstream.

LETHAL BLEEDING FEVER

The first known outbreak of Ebola occurred in 1976, in a mission hospital in the Democratic Republic of Congo. The virus is highly infectious, transmitted through coughs, sneezes, blood, and saliva. It causes a quick and painful death, during which the person bleeds from the eyes, nose, and gums, often with bloody vomiting and diarrhea, too. There is no known treatment.

THE MOST DISFIGURING DISEASE

In olden days, lepers looked so frightening that they were kept isolated in leper colonies. Their skin became thick, pitted and discolored, covered with rashes, walnut-sized nodules, and ulcers. Nerve damage caused their faces to distort, and fingers and toes became clawed or "fell off" because of injury or infection. Amazingly, about 750,000 people a year still contract leprosy, but modern antibiotics can now control the disease and people don't get disfigured in the same way.

BREATHING PROBLEMS

Ondine's Curse (also known as Congenital Central Hypoventilation Syndrome) causes people to "forget" to breathe while they're asleep at night. To make sure they wake up the next morning, they have an airway cut into their windpipe and have to sleep every night attached to a mechanical device which "breathes" for them.

FLESH-EATING BACTERIA

This horrible infection – known as necrotizing fasciitis – attacks deep layers of skin and flesh. Within days of infection (usually through a wound), the bacteria spreads widely causing gangrene and pus deep below the skin's surface. The way to halt its speedy progress is to cut out the dead ("necrotic") flesh by surgery, and sometimes the affected area even has to be amputated.

RABID WAY TO GO

Around 55,000 people a year die from rabies, mostly in Africa and Asia, from getting bitten by an infected animal. "Rabere" is the Latin for "to be mad" and once the virus reaches the brain it causes hallucinations, terror, and eventually total delirium. Sufferers start crying uncontrollably and frothing through their paralyzed jaws. Death usually occurs in 2 to 10 days' time.

WORLD'S BIGGEST KILLER

Smallpox is reckoned to have killed more people than any other disease – up to 500 million during the 20th century alone. It's very contagious, causing high fever and nasty virus-filled pustules around the face, body, and even palms of the hands and soles of the feet. Thankfully, worldwide immunization has today virtually eradicated the disease.

A PLAGUE ON YOU!

The bubonic plague was an especially bloody and gruesome way to die: 3 to 7 days after being bitten by a rat flea carrying the disease, painful "buboes" – lymph nodes swollen with decomposing flesh – would arise in a person's armpits, groin, and neck. They'd start vomiting and even urinating blood, dying in awful pain as their flesh decayed and turned black before their eyes.

MISSING ORGANS

In order to dry out a dead body to make a mummy, the Ancient Egyptians would remove all the organs. Long hooks were pushed up the nostrils into the brain and rapidly wiggled about until the brain became a mushy liquid that could be drained out of the nose. Other organs were cut out and put in jars that were buried along with the mummy.

THE RISE OF THE MUMMY

The Ancient Egyptians believed that you could not enter the afterlife if you did not have a body, so they tried to preserve dead bodies by embalming them as "mummies." The bodies were dried out for 70 days, covered in a special potion, and wrapped in bandage-like fabric.

TRAPPED IN THE TOMBS

It wasn't only curses that were used to protect tombs from robbers. The tombs were often hidden in a maze of dark corridors in which robbers could become lost or trapped. The floors sometimes had hidden holes and trapdoors, while lethal wires were rigged up that could slice a person's head off. In 1944, a robber died when a stone coffin lid trapped his arm. Then the roof fell down and crushed him.

HORRIBLE MEDICINE

Egyptian medicine was really advanced for its time, but many of the treatments were disgusting, including using animal dung, fat taken from cats, and insects. Wearing a bag of mouse bones around the neck was thought to cure bed-wetting. Many people died because of the doctor's attempt to cure them rather than from the illness they had in the first place.

KHUFU THE CRUEL

Pharaoh Khufu was very cruel and brought misery upon Ancient Egyptian people. He considered other people's lives worthless and thought it was acceptable for them to die while building his pyramids. Once, when he heard that a magician could bring dead things back to life, he decided to kill a prisoner just so that he could see if the magician was telling the truth.

BURIED WITH PHARAOH

Sometimes the pharaohs were not the only dead people in the tombs. In the early days, some of their servants were killed too so that they could look after them in the afterlife. The pharaohs' favorite cats were also mummified and buried with them. Egyptians thought that cats were holy and would shave off their eyebrows in mourning if their cat died.

YUK!

IN MEDIEVAL TIMES, EGYPTIAN MUMMIES WERE GROUND INTO POWDER AND USED AS MEDICINE.

CURSE OF THE MUMMIES

Many Egyptian tombs were inscribed with curses to stop people looting the riches buried with the mummies. The tomb of Pennuit, the high priest of Pharaoh Ramses II, featured hieroglyphics which meant: "As for anybody who shall enter this tomb in his impurity, I shall wring his neck as a bird." Other tomb curses include: "He shall die from hunger and thirst" and "He shall be miserable and persecuted."

PYRAMIDS OF DEATH

Until the beginning of the 20th century, Pharaoh Khufu's pyramid, built in 2530BC and known as the Great Pyramid, was the largest structure in the world, but its only purpose was as a monument to death. Up to 25,000 laborers had to haul 6.5 million tons of stone to build it, and many of them died in the process.

MORE THAN 10,000 PEOPLE A YEAR DIE FROM LARGE ROUNDWORMS MOVING AROUND IN THEIR INTESTINES.

WORMS ON THE BRAIN

Old medical texts often mention extracting worms, beetles, or centipedes from the human brain. But what kind of insects are they talking about? When the brain of an Egyptian mummy was analyzed in 1984, it was found to have several cysts containing the dog tapeworm larvae, Taenia multicepts. One theory is that the larvae used people's brains as their hosts, much as they sometimes colonize sheep's brains nowadays. This would produce headaches, fits, and loss of vision – and when the skull was opened, the cysts packed with wriggling tapeworm larvae would emerge.

JIGGER FLEAS

Tiny female jigger fleas burrow headfirst into human skin, leaving their rear ends sticking out of an opening through which they breathe. They feed on human blood, and mate. In a week or so, they blow up to the size of a pea and lay around 100 eggs which drop out of the hole in the person's skin on to the ground. These nasty creatures, found in Africa, cause intense itching, pain, and infection mostly around the feet and lower legs, because they can only jump 20cm (8in) high.

WORMING AROUND

Parasites use other living animals as their home and source of food. One scary parasite that lives inside the human body is the tapeworm. You get it from eating the larvae in meat which has not been cooked properly. The larvae grow into adult worms that live coiled in the intestines and can be as long as 15m (49ft). Other kinds of tapeworm eggs hook themselves on to organs such as the lungs, liver, even the brain, where they grow into huge cysts and can rupture nastily, causing the body to go into shock.

FIERY SERPENTS

Guinea worms are gruesome human parasites picked up by drinking larvae-infected water in sub-Saharan Africa. These thin white worms live for a year within the body and grow to a horrific 90cm (3ft) long. Then their heads emerge from blisters on the skin. They have to be pulled out by wrapping them round a stick or piece of cloth. This process can take a month or more and causes intense burning and pain – which is why guinea worms are nicknamed "fiery serpents."

MONSTROUS MUSEUM

Jars of weird and wacky parasites line the walls of the Meguro Parasitical Museum in Meguro, Tokyo, Japan. There's an 8.8m (28ft) long tapeworm, which once lived happily in a man's intestines, and hundreds of other slitherers, wigglers, and crawlers – some still inside the animals they infected.

GRUESOME SWELLINGS

One tiny worm is carried to humans in mosquito bites – and it causes a gruesome disease called elephantiasis, where the legs and other parts of the body swell up horribly, sometimes to 10 times their size. It's called the filarial worm and it can live in the body for up to 6 years.

WEE FISH

Candiru, or vampire fish, are small bloodsuckers that live in the Amazon River and were thought to swim up people's urinary tracts. Even as recently as 1997, a man said he was peeing standing in the river when a candiru jumped into his penis and swam up the tube that leads to his bladder. Swimmers in the Amazon are often warned not to wee in the water, just in case it allows the parasitic fish to enter the body.

DEATH BY ELEPHANT

It must have been very unnerving to see a war elephant in full armor charging toward you. So full marks to Eleazar Maccabeus who bravely threw himself beneath one at the battle of Beth-Zechariah in 162BC. He plunged his spear into the huge beast's belly – and the elephant fell down dead on top of him, crushing him to death.

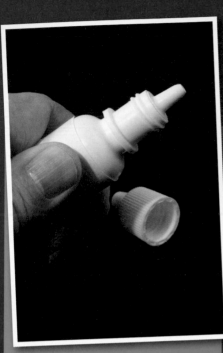

DEATH BY BOTTLE CAP

At the time of his death in 1983, it was reported that U.S. playwright Tennessee Williams had died by choking on the cap of his eyedrops bottle. Whenever he used the drops, he'd apparently lean back with the cap in his mouth, and drop the liquid into his eye, a method that proved fatal.

YUK! KING GEORGE II OF ENGLAND DIED OF A SWELLING IN HIS ARTERY, AFTER STRAINING ON THE TOILET!

FATAL JUMP

French tailor Franz Reichelt designed an extraordinary flying suit which doubled as a parachute. He'd tested it out on dummies several times from the top of his Paris apartment block, but wanted a bigger challenge. So in 1912 he decided to jump off the Eiffel Tower while wearing it. Unfortunately, the parachute failed to open and he landed on the ground below, dead on impact. Perhaps unsurprisingly, his suit never took off.

DEATH BY PUDDING

King Adolf Frederick of Sweden was a bit of a glutton, but he excelled himself one night in 1771. After a massive meal of traditional Swedish food such as smoked herring, caviar, seafood, and sour cabbage, he wolfed down his favorite pudding called semla, a sweet bun cut in half, stuffed with marzipan and cream, and soaked in hot milk. Some reports say he ate not 1 or 2 of these puddings, but a whopping 14! Whatever the truth, he died of digestive problems soon after and is renowned in Sweden as "the king who ate himself to death."

STRANGLED BY SCARF

U.S. dancer Isadora Duncan was strangled by her trademark long scarf in 1927. She was a passenger in an open-topped car on the French Riviera, her scarf flying behind her, but it became entangled with the car's open-spoked wheel and pulled her so hard it broke her neck.

PAIN IN THE BUTT

Humphrey de Bohun met a particularly gruesome end. In 1322, at the Battle of Boroughbridge in England, he led his rebel forces on to a wooden bridge to meet the enemy – and promptly got skewered by an iron pike through his bottom. It had been pushed upward through a gap in the planks by a royalist pikeman with a good aim, who'd been hiding below the bridge.

OFF WITH HER HEAD

When Mary Queen of Scots was beheaded in 1587, it was a disaster from start to finish. It took three swipes of the executioner's axe to sever her head from her body – the third time to cut through a tough bit of gristle. When the executioner held up her head to the assembled throng, her wig promptly fell off and, to everyone's horror, the short grey hair of an old woman was revealed. Then Mary's dog was found in the skirts of her headless body. The distraught hound raced to lie at the top of the Queen's severed shoulders, got covered in her spurting blood, and had to be dragged off and washed.

SUPER TONGUE

The chameleon lizard has a slivering tongue that can be longer than its entire body. The longest ones are a shocking 68.5cm (27in) long, which is a huge amount of tongue. It is incredibly quick, shooting out of its mouth and hitting its victim in just 0.03 of a second. The tip of the tongue is a muscular suction cup, covered in mucus. Small insects get stuck on the tongue and are sucked inside the chameleon's mouth and crushed by strong jaws before they know what has hit them.

GRUESOME MOLE

The blind, grotesque-looking star-nosed mole, which lives in the northeastern United States and Canada, has the most repulsive nose in the world. It has 22 squirming pink tentacles around it nose, as if a sea anemone had become stuck on its face. Yuk!

SUPER-LONG FINGER

The peculiar aye-aye looks like it has been stitched together from the body parts of other animals. It has big ears, bug-eyes, rodent-like teeth, and an enormously long, thin, middle finger. It taps on trees to locate grubs, gnaws a hole, and pokes its finger in to get at them. The aye-aye looks so strange that it is an omen of death for some in its native Madagascar.

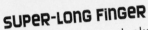

BIGGEST EYES

The colossal squid has the largest eyes of any living creature. The squid can grow up to 14m (46ft) long and its eyes can be 20in (51cm) in diameter. It uses its huge eyes to see in the dark depths of the oceans around the Antarctic. It needs to watch out for sperm whales, which are willing to brave the hooks on the squid's huge tentacles in order to kill and eat it.

YUK!
POLAR BEARS CAN GO THE WHOLE WINTER WITHOUT GOING TO THE TOILET ONCE.

HALF SEAHORSE, HALF TREE!

The leafy sea dragon has to be one of the weirdest-looking creatures in the world. Its body is much like that of a normal seahorse, but it has branches growing out of its sides! These leaf-like protrusions mean that it is brilliant at camouflaging itself and it can move through the water disguised as seaweed, ready to attack its prey of plankton and crustaceans.

FUNNY DUCK

The platypus is an evolutionary oddity. It is the only mammal that lays eggs rather than giving birth to its young. It also looks very peculiar. It has the bill of a duck, the feet of an otter, and the tail of a beaver. When it was first discovered, some scientists thought that it was a fraud that had been stitched together from the parts of other animals.

SLOW SLOTH

The sloth hardly ever moves. It likes to hang upside down from branches and doesn't do anything quickly. It takes up to a month to digest a meal and only gets down from the tree once a week to go to the toilet. It moves so little that its fur gets moldy, becoming covered with green algae.

COOKED CAPTAIN

In the 18th century, Captain Cook became the first person to map Canada's Newfoundland, most of Australia, and New Zealand. The Englishman's great adventures came to an end when he upset some native Hawaiians. Things turned nasty when they stole one of his boats, so he attempted to take their king hostage. Cook was struck on the back of the head and stabbed to death. The Hawaiians then baked his corpse.

FATHER AND SON LOST

Percival Fawcett was a British archaeologist who, in 1925, set out with his son in search of "Z," a lost city he believed existed in the Mato Grosso region of Brazil. They were last reported crossing the Upper Xingu, a tributary of the Amazon River, before disappearing forever. Many believe they were brutally killed by tribes whose territory they were entering, though they may have died of some dreadful disease. Over 100 would-be rescuers have died in several expeditions sent to uncover Fawcett's fate.

LOST IN THE OUTBACK

In 2006, Ricky McGee, who had been robbed and left for dead, was lost for 71 days in the remote desert of the Australian Outback. He had no food or water so had to survive on a diet of leeches, frogs, and insects. When he was finally found, he was virtually a skeleton, having lost 47kg (125lb) during his horrendous ordeal.

EVEREST DEATH TOLL

Hundreds of people have tried, failed, and died in horrible circumstances while climbing Mount Everest. Most of the deaths occur on the way down, after the victim has successfully reached the summit. Over 200 people have died, including 15 in 1996, and at least 120 dead bodies have been left on the slopes. Climbers sometimes find bits of rotting corpses or bones while they are making their ascent.

NUCLEAR SURVIVAL

Tsutomu Yamaguchi managed to survive the devastating explosions of not 1 but 2 nuclear bombs. On 6 August 1945, he was in Hiroshima, Japan, when the "Little Boy" atomic bomb was dropped on the city. He suffered burns but was well enough to return to his home city of Nagasaki, where the "Fat Boy" atomic bomb exploded 2 days later. Over 200,000 people died in the 2 attacks, but Mr. Yamaguchi only suffered minor injuries.

MOUNTAIN DISASTER

Joe Simpson survived a horrific ordeal when he broke his leg while up a 6,000m (19,700ft) mountain in the Peruvian Andes. His fellow climber, Simon Yates, tried to lower him down the mountain using a rope, but Simpson became stuck while hanging over the precipice. To save himself, Yates was forced to cut the rope, sending Simpson to almost certain death. Amazingly, he survived a 30m (100ft) fall, managed to get down the mountain, and crawled for 3 days with his smashed leg back to base camp.

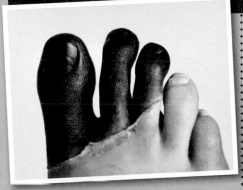

POLE DEATHS

Englishman Captain Scott and his team of four men endured terrible hardship and freezing cold as they attempted to become the first people to reach the South Pole in January 1911. They finally made it, but found out that the Norwegian Roald Amundsen had got there before them. On the torturous return march, they suffered frostbite, snow blindness, exhaustion, and hunger. They all died before they could make it home.

SANITARY SHOWERS?

About 45% of people in one study said they peed in the shower, but how sanitary is it? When wee is made in the kidneys there are no germs in it, but on the way out through the urinary tract it can pick up lots of bacteria and other nasty stuff, to which shower-wee-ers are exposing themselves!

WARMING WEE

In cold waters, divers often pee in their wetsuits. Wetsuits work by keeping a thin layer of liquid between the skin and the tight-fitting rubber suit, which heats up like a warm water blanket. But when water is cold, icy new flushes keep hitting the skin, so divers quickly get cold. They wee in their suits to raise the temperature of the liquid around them, and keep themselves warm.

WEE GARGLE

The Ancient Romans used pee as a mouthwash. In AD1, a physician called Dioscorides recommended swilling it round the mouth to make teeth whiter. Urine contains ammonia, which is a strong germ-killer. So, although it would have tasted vile, the Romans' breath might have smelled a bit sweeter afterwards.

WHAT'S POOP MADE OF?

Three-quarters of a human poop is water, but the rest is made up of 3 different things. There's fiber, the stuff in plants that our gut can't digest, but which keeps poo moving along the intestines. There are dead bacteria – these help digest food in the gut but turn into corpses in the process. Then there are other waste products – the fats, salts, mucus, and dead cells that our bodies can't use. Diarrhea is watery poo that moves really fast through your system. Whereas hard, dried-up turds have taken longer to get through the gut, so the water in them has been absorbed.

UGH!
EVERY TIME YOU SNEEZE, YOU RELEASE ABOUT 20,000 DROPLETS OF SALIVA AND MUCUS!

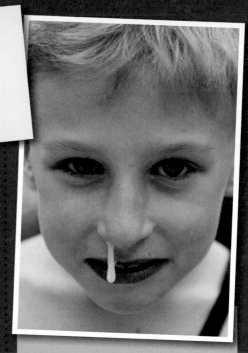

SPACEY PEE
On U.S. spacecraft, astronauts drink water that is made from their wee and sweat. Scientists found a way of recycling the perspiration taken from the cabin atmosphere with the astronauts' distilled urine, and making it into decent-tasting drinking water with a hint of iodine, a chemical used in the processing.

BLISTERING HECK!
Have you ever wondered what that thin clear fluid is in a blister? It's not water, it's serum, what's left of blood after the red blood cells and other things have been removed. Serum is packed with good things including proteins and antibodies that help the damaged skin repair. It also acts like a big fluffy pillow to protect the skin below. Eventually it's absorbed back into the body and disappears.

BOOGIE ON
The slimy snot that comes out of your nose is amazing stuff. It's called mucus and helps trap dust and bacteria before they can enter your lungs. It's mostly made up of water so it acts like a shower inside your nose, washing out loads of dead skin, dirt, and white blood cells that have died battling the bacteria. When you have a cold, you produce a lot of mucus which is busy expelling all the germs and dead blood cells. But sometimes snot dries out inside your nose, creating boogies. Don't eat them – these are hardened bits of dead germs and dirty salty stuff that you've breathed in.

SUMO LIFE

There's only one sport where people aim to gain as much body fat as possible – Sumo wrestling. Sumo is the national sport of Japan, and the aim is to bounce your opponent out of the ring, so hefty wrestlers have the advantage. Sumos eat enormous quantities of a high-calorie stew called "chanko-nabe" made of fish, meat, tofu, and vegetables. One wrestler called Konishiki (say it "Co–neesh-ki") who weighed 286kg (630lb) would typically eat 10 bowls of chanko, 8 bowls of rice, over 100 pieces of sushi, and 25 portions of fried beef at every meal. After eating, Sumos always take a long nap which helps their bodies lay down the food as fat.

PORKY FIGHTERS

Roman gladiators weren't lean hungry killing machines – in fact they were usually a little overweight. Forensic archaeologists who've studied their bodies found that they had very well-developed, dense bones in their arms, legs, and feet and ate a diet of barley-based vegetarian food which made them porky. This fatty layer would protect nerves and organs but would bleed dramatically when cut, giving spectators a harmless but gory thrill.

BACK BREAKING

U.S. team skier Dane Spencer was racing downhill in 2006 when he plunged off a 100ft (30.5m) ski jump called the Launching Pad. He shattered 2 vertebrae in his back, had massive internal bleeding, a broken pelvis, and was unconscious for 5 days. Eight months after surgery that permanently moved his windpipe, carotid artery, and jugular vein, he got back on the ski slopes and started training hard. By the next ski season, he'd returned to the national A ski team!

SPACE MARATHON

In 2007, NASA astronaut Sunita Williams ran the Boston marathon – in space. She completed the 42.16km (26.2 miles) on a treadmill while working on the International Space Station in orbit round Earth. It was much tougher than running on the ground. She was strapped to the treadmill by bungee cords in case she floated away, and had to catch the oranges that co-astronaut Oleg threw at her while running to try and relieve her thirst.

STICKING HIS NECK OUT

Manchester City goalkeeper Bert Trautmann saved the day in the 1956 FA Cup final, the most famous soccer competition in the UK. Diving at a ball, he got kicked in the neck and was knocked unconscious. No substitutes were allowed, so Trautmann got up and played on. He looked extremely dazed and giddy, but made some spectacular saves to lead his team to victory. That night, he couldn't move his head. Doctors discovered he had dislocated 5 neck vertebrae, and one was broken completely in half. He was lucky to be alive.

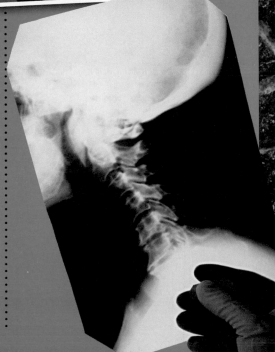

TYPHOID MARY

A single person was responsible for 53 cases of typhoid and 3 deaths in New York in 1907. Mary Mallon was a cook who carried the disease and spread it to her customers. She was put into quarantine for 26 years.

CHINESE DEATHS

The worst plague in recent centuries was called the "Third Pandemic." Like the Black Death, it was a bubonic plague carried by rodents. It started in China in 1855 and killed up to 12 million people over 100 years, when it finally died out.

THE WORST PLAGUE

In 1340, the Black Death came from Asia to Europe and killed half of the entire population. It may have been carried by fleas that lived on rats and then bit humans. The plague's symptoms included disgusting, black, smelly boils and a fever. Most people died within 48 hours. It reached Britain in 1348 and had killed more than a third of the population by the following year. Up to 50 million people died in Europe.

GREEKS IN A STATE

While the Ancient Greek city-state of Athens was fighting the Peloponnesian War against Sparta in 429BC, it suffered a typhoid epidemic which became known as the Plague of Athens and changed the course of history. About a third of the city's population, including its military leader, Pericles, was wiped out by the disease. Many people refused to help the victims because they were scared of catching the disease, so they were left to die. Athens eventually lost the war.

NEWCOMERS' DISEASE

Some of the worst epidemics in history happened in America. The native peoples of both North and South America had no immunity to some of the diseases brought over the Atlantic by European settlers from the 16th century onward. The Incas, the Aztecs, and many Native American tribes lost millions of their people to diseases like measles and smallpox.

THE GREAT STINK

In the summer of 1854, 600 Londoners died from cholera within just a couple of weeks. The cholera was carried in contaminated water. London did not have a hygienic sewage system. The city was often smelly and suffered a series of terrible epidemics of cholera. The summer of 1858 became known as "The Great Stink" because of the horrific stench that came from sewage during the unusually hot weather. A new sewage system wiped out the smell and the cholera.

DISEASED SHIP

The Great Plague of Marseille, which caused the death of 100,000 people, is believed to have been brought to the French port on just one ship in 1720. The merchant ship stopped off at plague-infested Cyprus and some of its sailors caught the disease. The merchants of Marseille knew that the boat was carrying the disease, but they were desperate for its prized cargo of silk and cotton so they let it dock. Within days, thousands of corpses lined the streets.

THE GREAT PLAGUE

In 1665, up to 100,000 people were killed by the Great Plague of London in a single year. It was carried by fleas, perhaps on ships that came from the Netherlands which had suffered a similar plague immediately before. If a member of a family caught the plague, their house was sealed, which meant that all the occupants inside would probably die. At night, corpse collectors would shout "Bring out your dead." The bodies would be taken away on carts and put in a plague pit.

DEADLY VIRUS

OTTER VS. CAIMAN

Most people think otters look cute, but don't be fooled. When river otters cannot find enough fish to eat they go into a mad frenzy and even gang up on fierce-fighting black caimans, 3 times their own size. Black caimans are the largest member of the alligator family, growing up to 4.2m (14ft), and have powerful snapping jaws. The otters, made fearless by hunger, attack them from above and below, rapidly swiveling, turning, and biting until the caiman becomes exhausted and can be killed.

THE ULTIMATE SCAVENGER

The hyena, which looks like a vicious, large spotted dog, has bone-crushing teeth and was seen as the ultimate scavenger of the Old World. Hyenas have been roaming the Earth, ravaging their prey, for 26 million years! One ancient species had teeth that could even crush elephant bones. They use teamwork to kill their prey and will even attack lions. They are also known for their habit of scavenging human graves for food.

TOP DOG

Wolves will attack and slay prey up to 10 times their own size, including cattle, horses, and huge American bison. A bison is more likely to survive if it stands its ground. If it runs, the wolves will chase it and bite its haunches, causing huge blood loss. Wolves also attack bear cubs and sometimes successfully chase away the cub's mother.

KILLER SHEEP

Bharals, also called Himalayan blue sheep, live high in the mountains of Asia. As soon as they are old enough, male bharals use their curved horns to push each other off cliffs and down mountains. They kill so many of their own kind that only half the males live to be 1 year old.

WHALE VS. SHARK

The orca, otherwise known as the killer whale, is so large and fearsome that it has no known predators. Its greatest battles are with large sharks including the smooth hammerhead, which at 5m (16ft) long is almost the same length as a killer whale. Orcas hold the sharks upside down so that they become powerless to defend themselves. In one filmed incident an orca killed a great white shark and then ripped out and ate its liver.

WOW! POLAR BEARS SUDDENLY ATTACK GROUPS OF WALRUSES AND EAT THE YOUNG CALVES THAT ARE CRUSHED IN THE PANIC.

SIAMESE FIGHTERS

Two male Siamese fighting fish should never be put in the same fish tank. The multicolored fish may look beautiful, but they are savage. They will attack each other, biting and tearing their fins, as soon as they see each other. Siamese fighting fish will even attack their reflection in a mirror.

MAN VS. BULL

Bullfighting remains a common form of entertainment in Spain. The bulls may be over 500kg (1,100lb), fast, and have sharp horns, but they are often no match for the trained matadors, who ceremoniously kill the bulls with a sword at the end of the fight.

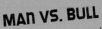

FAT FIGHT

Huge male elephant seals fight viciously with each other in order to win a mate. They charge, thump, and bite each other in an extreme battle which can last about 15 minutes. They weigh as much as an elephant (2,700kg/6,000lb) so it's best to get out of their way if they charge each other. The prize for the winner can be 50 females.

New Teeth for Old

Ancient people used to chomp through so much meat and tough vegetation that their teeth quickly wore down. So they were very glad when a new set of whopping molars arrived in their late teens. Today we all eat softer food so our other teeth survive for decades, and we don't need these useless extra "wisdom teeth." Often, there's not enough room in our mouths for wisdom teeth, so they grow in crooked or squash all our other teeth together, causing lots of trips to the dentist and gruesome pullings-out!

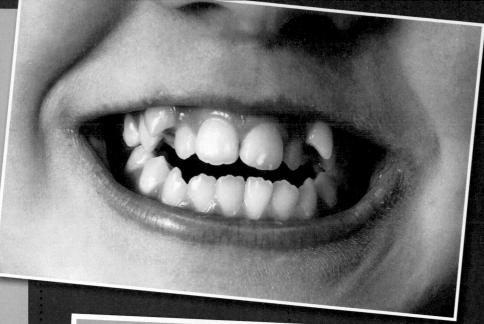

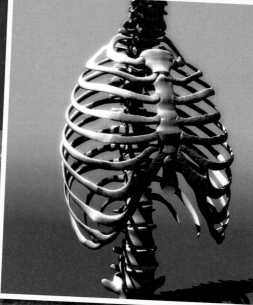

Odd Bods

Some people's bodies are littered with weird extra bits that were useful a very long time ago when we were grunting, scratching apes. One in 500 people has an extra rib – probably left over from the age of reptiles – at the top of their ribcage. The trouble is, this extra rib can squeeze a major artery and prevent the arm from working properly, so sometimes has to be removed. Others have an extra-strong muscle under their collarbone which makes them especially good at walking on all fours, while others have a muscle in their lower arm which is very helpful when they need to swing through trees or give themselves a big ape-like underarm scratch!

Goose Bumps

Humans used to be covered with thick pelt-like fur and could puff it up to make themselves look bigger and stronger or just to keep warm. Our fur has long gone, but amazingly we can still make our body hair stand on end – it's called goose bumps!

WOW!
AIR-FILLED SINUS BONES MAKE OUR HEADS LIGHTER TO CARRY AROUND!

TAILBONE TALES

Amazingly, human embryos have a tail when they're about 30 days old, though it disappears as they grow bigger. Our ape-like ancestors had proper tails and we still retain a bit of the tailbone – it's called the coccyx (say it "cock-six"), the last 4 or 5 vertebra at the bottom of the backbone. Occasionally, there are still people born today with real tails, such as Chandre Oram from India whose tail is an astonishing 33cm (13in) long.

MOVING EARS

Dogs, cats, rabbits, and deer can make their ears prick up, and our ape-like ancestors could probably make their ears move independently of their head, too. Even now, one in 10 people has a tiny prominent area of thicker skin on the top ridge of their ear. This is the remnant of a larger, folded-over ear that people could move in order to listen more clearly to distant sounds.

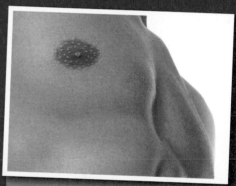

THIRD EYELID

Cats, dogs, birds, sharks and lizards have a transparent third eyelid which flicks across the eye to moisten or protect it – in fact, the woodpecker's third eyelid stops its eyeballs falling out when it bashes its beak against a tree! Humans have the remnants of a third eyelid, too. It's quite small, hidden away in the inner corner of the eye near the tear ducts. It doesn't flicker across the eyeball any more, but it does produce that yucky crusty substance called "sleep" in your eyes every morning.

THIRD NIPPLE

The weirdest and most useless human body part is probably the "third" nipple. Amazingly, 1 in 18 people have one, though it often looks more like a mole than a nipple. Third nipples are usually found on the "milk lines," vertical lines of slightly thickened skin which lead from the armpit down to the pelvis – though in Brazil in 2006, one person was found with a well-formed nipple on the sole of their foot!

DUMB SUPPER

If you ever come across a mock table setting for two on top of a grave or tomb, don't disturb it – someone's been having dinner with the dead! The dumb supper is an old ritual often held on Hallowe'en. The living provide the plates, glasses, and cutlery, and eat an imaginary meal backward while having a silent chat with their ghostly ancestors.

MYSTERY MAN

Macabre mystery writer Edgar Allan Poe died in very mysterious circumstances and was buried not once but twice in Westminster Grounds and Burying Hall in Baltimore (he was moved to a better position). His unsettled ghost is said to visit the graveyard every year on January 19th wearing a black fedora hat, scarf, and coat and carrying a walking stick with a silver cat's head on it.

VOODOO MOANING

The ghost of voodoo priestess Marie Laveau is said to haunt St. Louis Cemetery in New Orleans. People say she wanders around the ornate tombs wearing a red and white turban, proclaiming voodoo curses so loudly that they can be heard on the neighboring street. Her two familiars – a boa constrictor called Zombie and a glowing red-eyed black cat – are also said to prowl around her vault, guarding it day and night.

UNDERGROUND UPSETS

The Paris catacombs, chilly dark passageways that lie deep beneath the city's streets, are said to be one of the most haunted places in the world. Here, the skeletons of centuries of Parisians are stored, their skulls and bones carefully arranged against the walls. Visitors often believe they are followed round the catacombs by groups of ghostly apparitions, which stand still and silent behind them, waiting patiently for them to move on.

GHOSTLY LICKS

Kabar the Great Dane is a very friendly doggie ghost who is said to lick the hands of people who stop beside by his grave in the Los Angeles Pet Cemetery. He belonged to silent movie star Rudolph Valentino and was buried in 1929.

NASTY EFFLUVIA!

Cholera was thought to be spread by "effluvia," an invisible vapor or gas that emanated from its dead victims. To stop the vapor leaking out, diseased bodies were meant to be buried at least 2m (7ft) deep. But in the 19th century, cemeteries were often so full that it was impossible to dig more than 1m (3ft) without coming across layers of older bodies in various stages of decomposition. Not a job for the faint-hearted!

SAVED BY THE BELL

The Huguenot cemetery in St. Augustine, Florida is said to be full of spooks and phantoms, and ghost lights and ectoplasm have been captured on camera. It's thought this supernatural activity is the result of so many people being buried alive here. In the 1880s, a yellow fever epidemic hit town, and people were so worried about catching the deadly disease that they'd inter the victims while they were in a coma. Richer families would attach a bell to their buried relative's hands, just in case they woke up and needed help to get out.

THE SAVING BELL (JUST IN CASE!)

TUMULTOUS TOMB

Wealthy Thomas Chase bought a burial vault in Barbados that was half underground. But every time it was opened for another family member to be buried, all the other coffins inside were found to have been moved, sometimes completely upended. This happened 5 times within 8 years, until the vault was sealed by local officials who wanted to discover what was going on. When it was reopened a few months later, it's said that all the coffins inside were topsy-turvy once more, and that the bony arm of one of Chase's daughters, Dorcas, was sticking out of the side of her coffin. The family never used the vault again.

WOW! A TAPHOPHILIAC (SAY IT "TAR-FO-FIL-IAC") IS SOMEONE WHO ADORES VISITING CEMETERIES AND GRAVES.

NOURISHING VIPERS

Theriac was the most fashionable medicine from Roman times to the 17th century, used as a cure-all for everything from plagues to pestilence. It was a mix of more than 50 plants, roots, and resins but with one essential ingredient – powdered dried viper. Theriac was hugely expensive so only rich people could afford it, but they used to eat big chunks of it daily, just as we take vitamin tablets today.

TAR WATER CRAZE

George Berkeley was not a doctor. In the 1740s, though, he wrote a book about the health benefits of drinking a gruesome brew called tar water. He thought drinking a pint a day would cure just about every health problem including smallpox and ulcerated bowels. Tar water was made by mixing pine tree tar with water, allowing it to settle for 48 hours, then draining off the water. He set off a health craze that became hugely popular round the world, even though it was useless medicinally.

SMART AS MUSTARD

Mustard seed is very hot to the taste, and just as powerful when put on the skin. Mustard plasters were often used to treat chesty coughs, bronchitis, and pneumonia – it was thought that bringing heat and blood to the area would work as a cure. The seed was mashed into a poultice, laid on a layer of protective cotton over the chest, and left for just 20 minutes. Any longer and skin could blister, burn, and ulcerate.

WACKY EAR CURES

To cure earache, people used to pour warm urine, pig's milk, baked onion juice, or the blood of a patent-leather beetle in their ears. They'd plug the opening with shelled snail, warm bacon, or garlic.

POXY PUSTULES

The Chinese used to protect themselves against smallpox by smearing a little fluid from the poxy pustules on to a wad of cotton and placing it in their noses. It may have smelled bad but as an early example of immunization, it probably worked.

TALL TAILS

Some ancient Egyptian cures probably worked quite well. They used to put moldy bread and honey on to infected wounds – mold kills bacteria and honey is a good antiseptic. But then they would put a live mouse on the gums of a toothache sufferer, believing that as mice had good teeth, perhaps the human would, too!

BLOODSUCKING LEECHES

Most fevers and illnesses were thought to be caused by too much fluid in the body, so doctors were forever bleeding their patients' of so-called "bad" blood. They often put black leeches – which can drink four times their weight in blood – on to people's skin, where they feasted until they grew so fat they fell off.

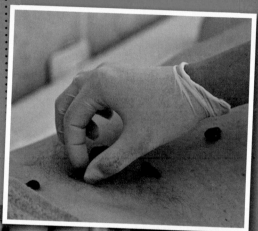

THE MAGIC OF TOADS

In the Middle Ages, toads were believed to have magical stones in their heads which worked as antidotes to poisons. The stones had to be extracted from the toad while it was alive and sitting on a red cloth, according to one 17th-century expert. These toadstones were set into rings which were meant to become extremely hot whenever poison was nearby, warning the wearer against eating whatever food or drink they were offered.

BLACK MAGIC

People thought the Black Death was spread by poisonous air, so to prevent themselves falling ill they wore bags of poo around their necks or took baths in urine, hoping the nasty smell would drive the poisons away.

POISONED BLOW DARTS

In the jungles of South America, native tribes hunt animals with blow darts dipped in curare poison. The poison, which is extracted from plants, paralyzes the animal, making it much easier to get close to it for the final kill.

POISON POTION

Signora Giulia Toffana made her living from poison. In 17th-century Italy, she produced Acqua Toffana (the "water of Toffana"), a toxic mix of arsenic, lead, and perhaps belladonna which was sold as a cosmetic and religious water. She used to sell her Aqua to wives who wanted to dispose of their rich husbands. It's thought the women were told to add the colorless liquid to their husband's wine during meals. Signora Toffana was finally caught and executed, but not before she'd sent an estimated 600 men to gruesome deaths by poison.

STINK BOMB

Scientist and inventor Leonardo da Vinci (1452–1519) designed a stink bomb containing sulfur and arsenic, to be used in warfare by his patron, the Duke of Milan. The chemicals were contained in a shell, to be fired from a cannon, and on landing would explode, releasing a cloud of very smelly and doubtless deadly poisons.

SATAN'S CHERRIES

The juicy berries of deadly nightshade – gruesomely nicknamed Satan's cherries – cause blurred vision, convulsions, paralysis, and even death when eaten by humans. But they have no effect whatsoever on birds. Many types of birds happily chomp on them and then disperse the seeds around the countryside in their poo. Horses, rabbits, and sheep also eat deadly nightshade's leaves with no ill effects.

CYANIDE SYMPTOMS

Being poisoned by cyanide is like hiking up a mountain at very high altitudes when there's not enough oxygen for the body to work properly. Victims feel weak, exhausted, short of breath, headachey, and confused. Their skin turns cherry red, their breath smells of bitter almonds, they breathe incredibly fast, and they often collapse after a short while with heart failure.

StRYCHNINE JITTERS

Thomas J. Hicks was running the Olympic marathon in 1904 when he began to flag a few miles from the end. But his trainers were determined he was going to win. So they gave him 2 separate doses of the deadly poison strychnine washed down with some brandy. Strychnine is a stimulant which contorts and contracts the muscles, so it gee-ed him over the finishing line. He won the gold medal, then promptly collapsed.

DEADLY SLEEP

In Shakespeare's play *Romeo and Juliet*, it was probably a potion of henbane that sent Juliet into a death-like sleep for 42 hours, turning so cold and still she hardly appeared to breathe. Henbane is a deadly poison which has a knock-out effect on the body, and in Elizabethan times was given to people suffering from insomnia. The trouble is with the dosage: a tiny bit too much and that person never wakes up.

SOCRATES

HEMLOCK HORRORS

Socrates was an Ancient Greek who was forced to take the poison hemlock in 399BC. He was a great thinker and it's believed he chose hemlock because, although it paralyzes the body, the mind remains clear, so he would know what was going on. The poison spreads slowly through the body, numbing toes and fingers first, then creeping into the limbs and body, where it paralyzes the lungs and breathing stops.

JACQUERIE REVOLT

In the 14th century, the French nobility pushed the peasants too far. The peasants were fed up with the way they were being treated. In 1358, they revolted and their actions were horrific, even torturing and killing women and children. The noblemen's response was violent. They slaughtered 20,000 peasants.

TIME OF CHAOS

The Dark Ages often refer to the time in European history between the fall of the Roman Empire in the 5th century and the rise of the Renaissance in the 14th century. Much of Roman civilization, law, and education were wiped away. Barbarians fought, pillaged, and caused chaos throughout Europe. Meanwhile, peasants had a very tough time.

CRUSADING CANNIBALS

Soldiers were usually just poor peasants made to fight for their lords. In a long campaign they would ransack the countryside to steal food, but sometimes they would not find enough. French soldiers in the First Crusade in 1098 were faced with starvation and decided to eat the enemy. One man wrote: "Our troops boiled pagan adults in cooking pots."

NEW BARBARIANS

From AD350, the Angles and the Saxons from northern Germany took advantage of the decline of the Roman Empire to spread across Europe and invade Britain. They were pagans who loved war in order to get rich and have slaves. The Saxon leader, Hengest, was savage, killing British bishops, priests, and peasants.

THE PEASANTS ARE REVOLTING

In 1381, English peasants decided to revolt. As a result of the Black Death there was a shortage of labor, so the peasants' masters made them work harder than ever and raised their taxes. Led by Wat Tyler, the peasants marched on London, stormed the Tower of London, and killed the Archbishop of Canterbury. Tyler was killed by the king's men, and the revolt was quashed. To stop another uprising, peasants were banned from leaving their villages.

POOR PEASANTS

During the Dark Ages, peasants were continually beaten, battered, and bruised by their masters, who could choose to kill them if they did anything wrong. Most people were incredibly poor and were not allowed to own anything. Everything belonged to their lord, who had complete power over them, and they had to work incredibly long hours farming his land while at the same time facing starvation.

HARSH JUSTICE

The peasants had no real rights. If they broke the law, the lord would decide their fate, and his punishments would be very harsh. The criminal would be whipped or dragged behind a galloping horse over rough ground. Sometimes, their head and hands would be put in stocks and people would throw things at them or beat them up while they were trapped.

MURDEROUS BURIALS

Like the Egyptians, the Saxons liked to bury servants alongside their deceased master. Many of them were not killed first, though: they were buried alive so they could serve their masters in the afterlife. Over the centuries, the Saxons converted to Christianity, stopped these burial practices, and led a more civilized way of life.

ELEPHANT MAN

Englishman Joseph Merrick's face and body were so deformed yet his character so thoughtful and intelligent that he became famous during Victorian times as the "Elephant Man." His face was lumpy, swollen, and badly misshapen, his right arm was the size of an elephant's front leg, and the skin on his body was thick, grey, and lumpy, just like an elephant's. Today scientists believe he had a very rare condition called Proteus syndrome, in which bones and skin grow freakishly unchecked.

WASP WAIST

Cathie Jung from Connecticut, U.S.A., is over the average height for women at 1.72m (5ft 8in) but she has a spookily tiny waist. At just 38.1cm (15in), it's about the circumference of a pineapple, making her look like a living Barbie doll. She's worn corsets for most of her life, sometimes for 24 hours a day, which helps accentuate her hour-glass figure.

BENDY SISTERS

The 3 Ross sisters – Aggie, Maggie, and Elmira – shot to fame in the 1940s with their singing, dancing, and contortion routines. They had extraordinary frontbending and backbending skills and could easily tuck their feet under their chins and waggle them – in triplicate! Their most famous routine was Solid Potato Salad from the 1944 MGM musical *Broadway Rhythm*, where their contortioning inside a big barn is truly gruesome.

LOBSTER FAMILY

Eight generations of the Stiles family of the U.S.A. have had lobster-shaped hands and feet. It's called Lobster Claw syndrome. Their middle finger is missing, and the rest of the hand is split in two, giving the appearance of lobster claws. It usually occurs in both hands and feet, and makes walking difficult. It's a genetic disorder called ectrodactyly (say it "ek-trow-dak-tilly"), and can also occur in frogs, toads, chickens, rabbits, and even cats and dogs.

ALLERGIC TO WATER

Australian Ashleigh Morris comes out in a painful rash and hives every time she gets wet. She has a rare condition which means she's allergic to water, so washing, swimming, and even sweating cause her body to explode in sore, itchy lumps – though they go down in a couple of hours. She always has an umbrella with her in case of rain!

SPONTANEOUS BLEEDING

Even though she's not hurt or cut in any way, Indian teenager Twinkle Dwivedi sometimes bleeds from her skin, feet, neck, hairline, and even her eyes. Doctors are baffled by her condition, though it's thought she might have a type of blood-clotting disorder that can be cured.

ROGUE HAND

In alien hand syndrome, a person's hand seems to have a mind of its own. It does things completely independently of its owner's wishes, like scratching, undoing zips, opening doors, tearing clothes – it sometimes even turns violent and tries to strangle its owner. People usually don't know what their hand is up to until someone else points it out, which is why they frequently say they feel the hand is possessed by a nasty alien force. Alien hand syndrome occurs after some kinds of brain surgery or injury.

MAN IN BOTTLE

Escapologists escape from things, but enter-ologists try to fit themselves into the tiniest spaces. One of the most spectacular is contortionist Hugo Zamoratte, an Argentinean who discovered in the 1970s that he could dislocate his joints. He can now reorganize his body so it squeezes into a big bottle, just like a genie!

PICTURE CREDITS